# FACADES:
## selection and details

Author: Pilar Chueca

© Carles Broto i Comerma
Jonqueres, 10, 1-5
08003 Barcelona, Spain
Tel.: +34 93 301 21 99
Fax: +34-93-301 00 21
E-mail: info@linksbooks.net
www.linksbooks.net

# FACADES:
## selection and details

# contents

STONE      8

REINFORCED CONCRETE AND BLOCKS      22

BRICKWORK      40

VENEER      58

RENDERED      70

WOODEN      84

METAL      110

GLASS      140

PLASTIC      168

MIXED      178

FACADE ENCLOSURES      200

# introduction

Facades no longer have to form part of the structure as loadbearing walls, but are a skin that wraps the building and gives it personality through the materials, textures, colours and compositions.

As external elements that are visible from outside the building, facades have reflected the cultural and aesthetic changes and the evolution of the customs of their users. One of the aspects that has marked the evolution of facades has been the discovery of new building materials such as concrete, which in the 20th century led to a definitive change towards specialisation and autonomy of the facade.

Facades are also to a certain extent the letter of introduction to the architectural work, the first thing we see. They may seduce us or make us despair, and through their reading one can imagine the nature of what is hidden behind them.

At present, though facades still in many cases show new, valid and attractive ideas, one of the main problems of contemporary architecture is the absence of an authentic system of industrialised facades that solves the functional requirements whilst conserving lightness and modernity.

Though there is an increasing number of specialists in walls and the production of mass-produced and tailor-made facades is increasing, there are still many technical aspects that must be resolved a posteriori. These aspects, often undervalued, are those that give validity to the design by solving the requirements of the facades.

Facades comprise part of the walls that make up a building, providing protection from the weather and the external environment. Therefore, this part of the building must meet requirements of habitability, stability and durability such as:

- Protection against the wind

- Expansion joints

- Respect for structural joints

- Acoustic insulation

- Thermal insulation

- Protection against moisture, including rain, snow and condensation.

# STONE FACADES

Initially there was no separation between the wall and the structure, and the wall was the only element that solved the problems of strength, water tightness and thermal insulation by being very thick.

The great thickness of old stone walls gives them good thermal behaviour, due to their ability to accumulate and give off heat (thermal inertia). Also, due to their great mass, they provide excellent acoustic insulation.

These traditional loadbearing walls have no reinforcement, so their flexural strength is very limited. There are two main types: rammed earth and rubble masonry.

Walls of rammed earth are made from worked clay that is poured into formwork. This system is common in areas where natural stone is scarce. The buildings may have up to three floors with a minimum thickness of 50 cm. Today this system is rarely used.

Rubble walls are made with rough stones laid by hand to fit together without courses or standard sizes. They can be made with cement or lime mortar, or dry.

The minimum thickness of the wall is 40 cm. These walls are very strong. There is no limit to their height, but their stability and settlement must be taken into account.

The limits of local construction are determined by the availability of local resources of stone or clay and even the climate conditions.

This construction solution has been abandoned over the course of time due to its great weight and thickness and the high cost of manpower.

The volumetric design adapts to the topography and tries to take advantage of visual perspectives. This explains the gently curving facades: on the west facade, the inflexion is marked by a vertical glazed strip that incorporates an element of contrast in its essentially opaque surface.

The selection of the materials is in harmony with both the typological context and the regulations: walls of stone rubble (with the two varieties that are characteristic of the location) and salvaged Arabian roof tiles.

The tension of the curves is used to establish several wall layers that differentiate the spaces.

Eduard Bru. Casa Cabani.

1. Copper cladding
2. Pine platform
3. Air chamber
4. Thermal insulation
5. Reinforced concrete panel
6. Existing granite masonry
7. Render
8. Air chamber
9. Beech wood floor
10. Beech wood frame
11. Beech wood staircase
12. Waterproof mortar
13. Existing rocky dike
14. Geotextile
15. Concrete wall
16. Gravel box
17. Pipe

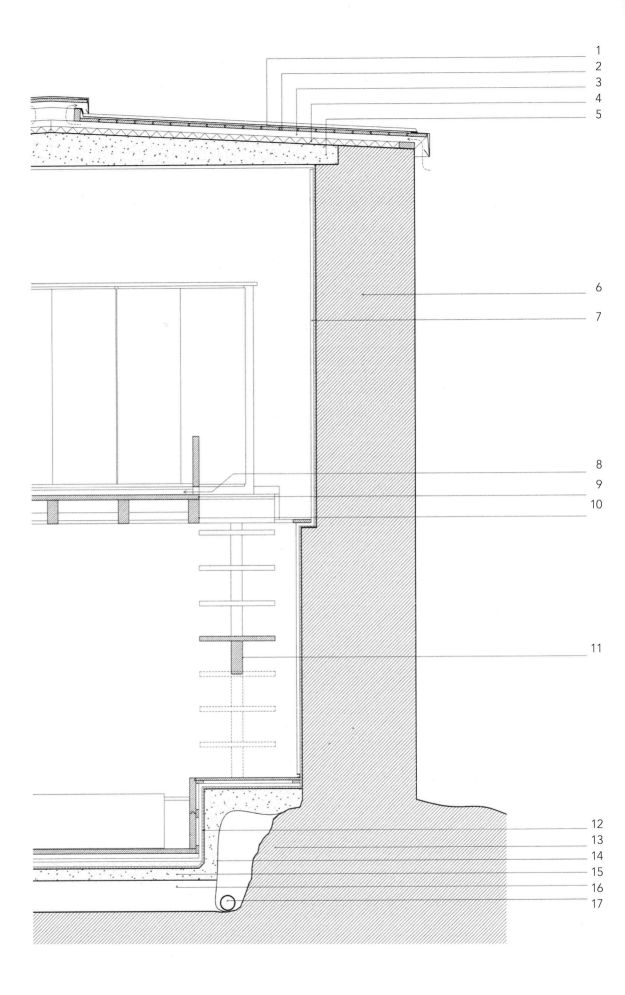

13

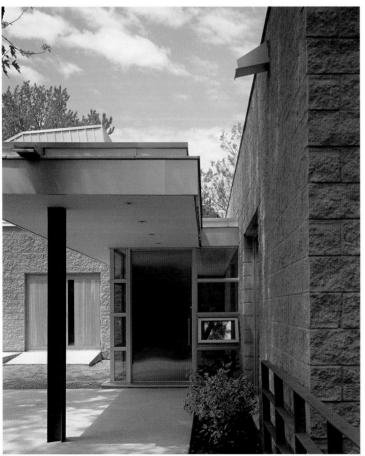

Bruce Kuwabara & Evan Webber. Residence and Studio in Richmond Hill.

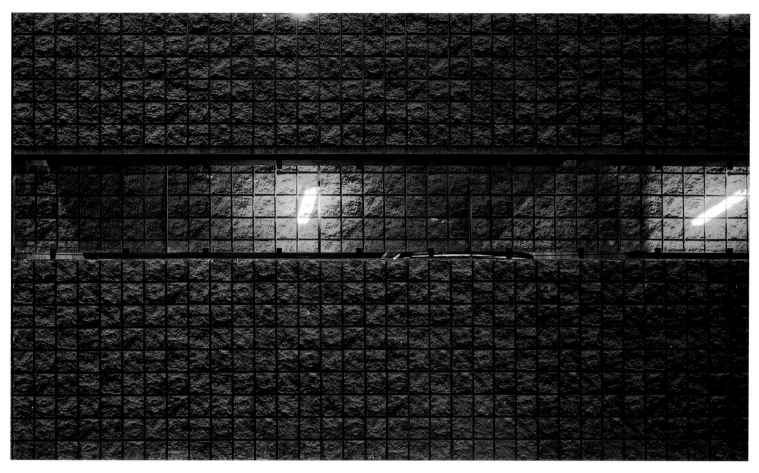

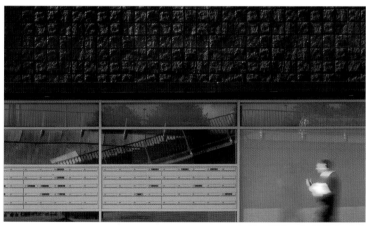

Wiel Arets Architect & Ass. Hoge Heren.

15

In this house two different levels are combined, each one with its own programme and aim, together with two different techniques used in the construction of these two levels. Indeed, two houses were conceived and built as one. The first level, for the children, consists of an opus incertum, a stone cube with doors and windows. The second level, for the parents, is a concrete cube with a large glazed balcony.

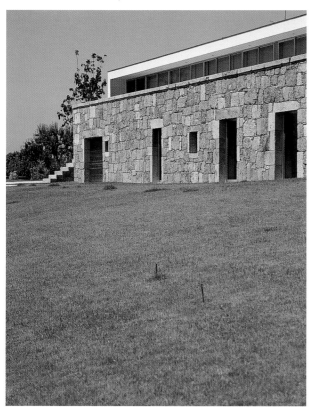

Traditional Lebanese architecture is invariably formed by a cube or a parallelepiped, with a flat roof or a pyramid-shaped roof of red tiles. In the centre of the main facade is a triple arcade that corresponds to the foyer and forms the main element of this residential unit. In this design scheme, it was important to preserve the volumetrics and the external treatment of the stone that is typical of Lebanese architecture, while at the same time changing the rigid pattern of the central foyer for a more flexible design. The design of the central foyer in the traditional architecture involves the use of a strict symmetry that is exteriorised in the treatment of the facade. The introduction of a loggia covered with a cross vault located at one end of the facade allowed the traditional triple arcade to be replaced, thus converting the facade into an asymmetric composition.

The use of stone allows the dwelling to adapt to the environment easily, and provides a reinterpretation of the local architecture. The climate requires the use of this material and a red-tile roof, because both elements can withstand the heavy snowfall in winter.

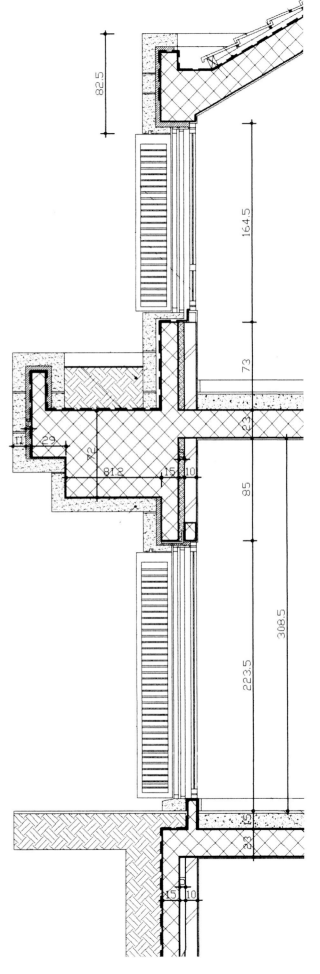

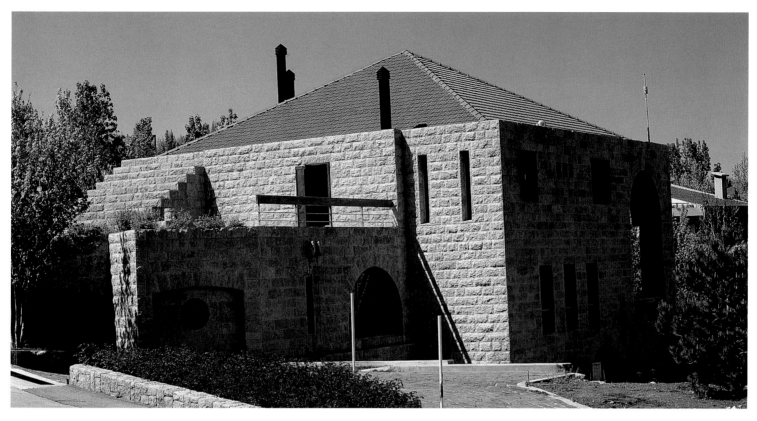

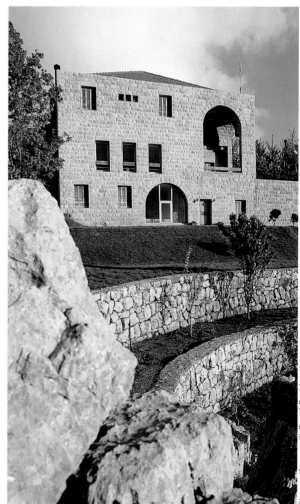

Simone Kosremelli. Fattal-Residence.

The materials used reinforce the main concepts behind the project: the stone shows moderation, the molded wood and aluminum soffits open to create cracks of light, the white from the walls on the upper floor blurs the boundaries and the glass allows nature to penetrate the different spaces.

Steven Harris Architects. House in Cabo San Lucas.

21

# FACADES OF REINFORCED CONCRETE AND BLOCKS

In theory, facades of reinforced concrete provide a simultaneous solution for the wall and the structure of the building. A single material provides water and air tightness and insulation. However, if these functions were to be met by concrete, the walls would be very thick, so thermal insulation and waterproofing are also used.

When the outer skin of the facade is concrete, one must bear in mind the thermal bridges that can be created when the thermal insulation is on the interior.

Blocks of exposed concrete and cement are used in buildings with up to four storeys above ground level in locations with seismic levels of less than 8. This structure of blocks of exposed concrete or cement follows the same criteria as a brickwork structure, though it may have reinforcement that allows cross walls to be replaced by bracing.

The blocks must have a very high quality surface and edges, regardless of the mortar that is used.

In addition to smooth blocks, there are a large variety of finishes. For double walls cavity walls, ties between the two walls are used.

For the outer facing one must choose blocks with a high quality surface and edges, whether one is using normal grey mortar, white cement and marble aggregate or coloured cement.

In addition to blocks with a smooth face, there is a wide range of possibilities for this technique, such as GER, Split, Diamante, Hi-lite, Rudolph, etc.

The bonding and the construction technique vary according to the type of block chosen.

The predominant geometry on the facade is the rectangle. This rhythm is determined by a linear succession of "solids" and "voids" in which the former act as private spaces and the latter act as an area for community life.

The private space is in turn divided into a porch and a room, so the differentiation between exterior and interior is slightly blurred.

The facades are composed of three differentiated elements that are used to provide functional and aesthetic qualities: reinforced concrete, glass and air.

Silvia Gmür & Livio Vacchini: 3 Single-Family Houses.

An enormous cracked wall of reinforced concrete is a silent witness to the former prosperity and the future possibilities not only of the hotel but of the whole area.

This museum consists of four blocks of concrete (exhibition halls) and water spaces. The museum is clad in reinforced concrete. The use of concrete for the exterior provides a sensation that the museum is elevated. The curved concrete wall expresses the scale of Mount Daisen. The purity of Takenaka was based on the abstraction and purity of the volumes and materials that were used: the four blocks of concrete compose a very forceful profile.

A single-family house built in reinforced concrete with a partial steel structure

On the exterior the most outstanding feature of the facade is the curvature of the wall on the left of the entrance.

The concrete was left unadorned in almost the whole dwelling as can be seen in the columns, thus complementing the mainly white plaster surfaces with touches of primary colours.

Rainer Köberl + Astrid Tschapeller. Supermarket MPREIS Wenns.

Denton & Corker & Marshall. Marshall House.

Zaha Hadid Architects. Phaeno Science Center Wolfsburg.

31

The structure of this dwelling consists of two parallel rows of post-stressed walls of concrete blocks, as if it were an artificial canyon that supports the concrete floor and ceiling. The north facade is open with 1.2 m wide pillars to provide as much natural lighting as possible for the interior. Glass panels are placed between the pillars, creating a distorted vision of the landscape.

On the other hand, the composition of the south facade avoids the sunlight with double-width pillars.

The concrete panels were sealed and polished to offer a shiny silver finish.

Wendell Burnette. Studio Residence in Sunnyslope.

Luis Ibarra & Teresa Rosano. Gracia House.

All of the blocks are of the same size and height, and covered with large panels of blue concrete, embedded with vitreous glass fragments.

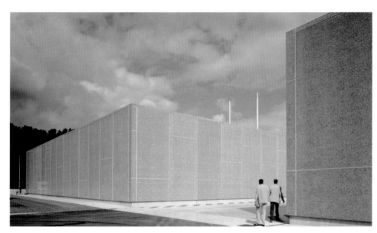

Jacques Ferrier Architecte. Sapeg water treatment plan.

35

# FACADES OF CEMENT BLOCKS

The main facade of this house serves as a formal and visual point of reference for the whole scheme.

This facade concentrates the whole expressive force of the building, formalised in a wall with a broken design that contains the main access and is defined by a characteristic feature: the striking arrangement of the greyish cement blocks that form a bond that plays with the reflected sunlight.

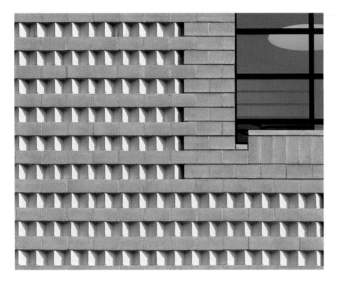

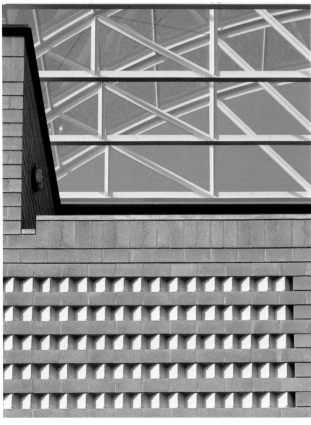

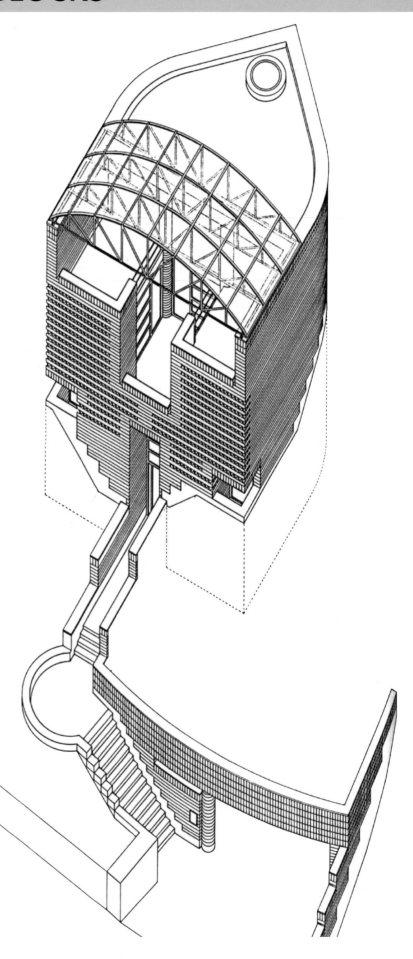

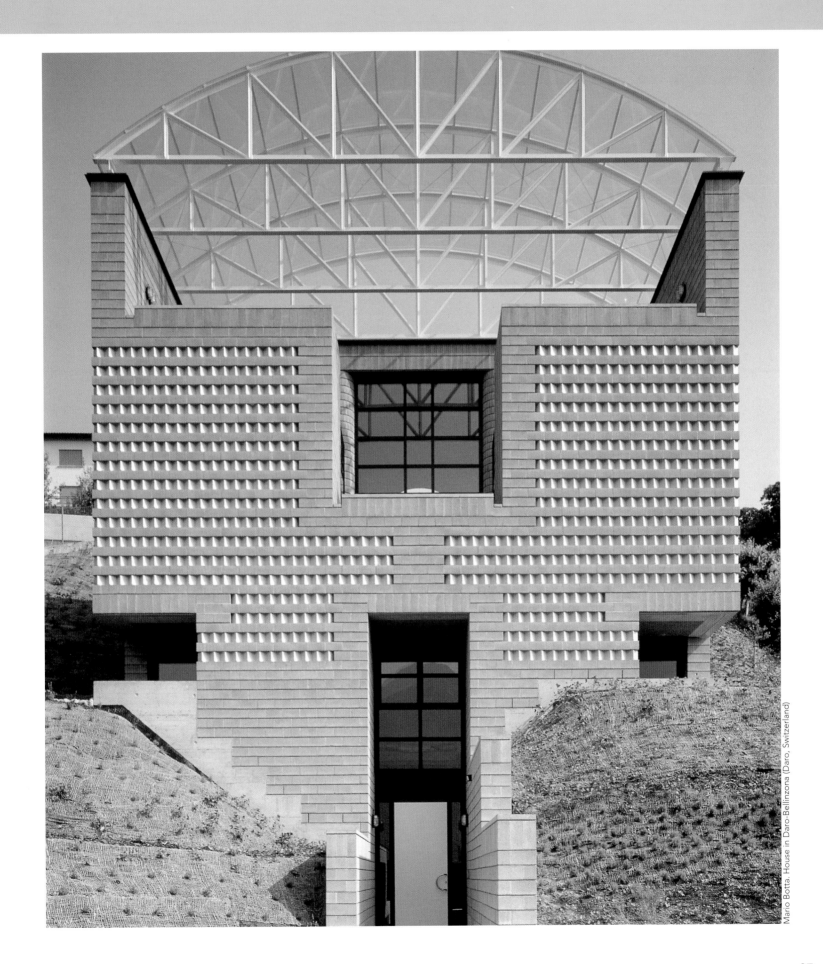

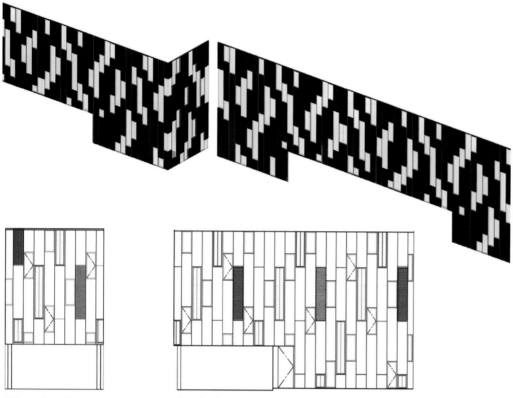

Rather than sealing the sides and bringing light into the house through the front and back elevations, the architects were determined to bring in sunlight on all four sides, resulting in a simple shape with 105 vertical slit windows positioned to frame the most desirable views.

A simple material, cement board, was used in conjunction with three types of glazing. The focus is on surface manipulation, with the architecture defined through the envelope of the volume rather than the volume itself. The design is based on a steel framed cube that makes maximum use of the 25 x 55 foot footprint and frees the skin from structural restraints, allowing an unrestricted rhythm of glazing, channel glass and solid panels.

West elevation

South elevation

Lorcan O'Herlihy Architects. Vertical House.

The selection of the façade materials corresponds to the nature of the building material underneath: concrete structural walls become side elevations, rendered and painted red; the brick front walls are clad in fibrous cement panels, installed in a vertical layout to enhance the façades verticality.

Dekleva Gregoric Arhitekti. Housing L.

# BRICK FACADES

The system used today to build facades of exposed brickwork is the result of a long process of variation of solid loadbearing walls. Exposed brickwork walls are considered as a traditional solution, so the image offered is that of traditional loadbearing walls.

The bricks used on these facades must be solid or perforated, standard size and top quality, to guarantee the colour and the absence of defects (stains, efflorescence, burns, etc.). Bricks of lower quality can be used provided that they do not have defects affecting more than 15% of the exposed surface. Machine-made bricks are now used exclusively. Hand-made bricks are no longer used.

The different types of exposed brickwork walls are:

- **Bonded walls**: These are bonded in their whole thickness and use a single type of brick There are different types of bond such as stretcher and header bonds (according to the face of the brick that is left exposed); English cross or St Andrew's cross, which alternate courses of stretchers and headers; Flemish or Dutch bond, which alternate stretcher and header bonds in the same course.

- **Walls with alternating courses**: these are bonded walls in which horizontal courses are alternated with masonry of another material.

- **Walls with piers**: these are bonded walls that have piers to provide greater strength.

- **Double walls**: These are built of the same or a different type of brick, and are interwoven by cramps, ties, alternating courses, etc.

- **Cavity walls**: these are double walls that are separated with a cavity between them.

The thickness and finish of the joints is very important to obtain the desired finish on the facade.

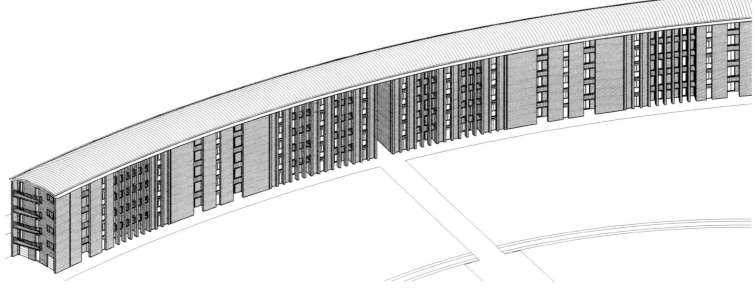

Massimo & Gabriella Carmassi. 48 apartments in Pontedera.

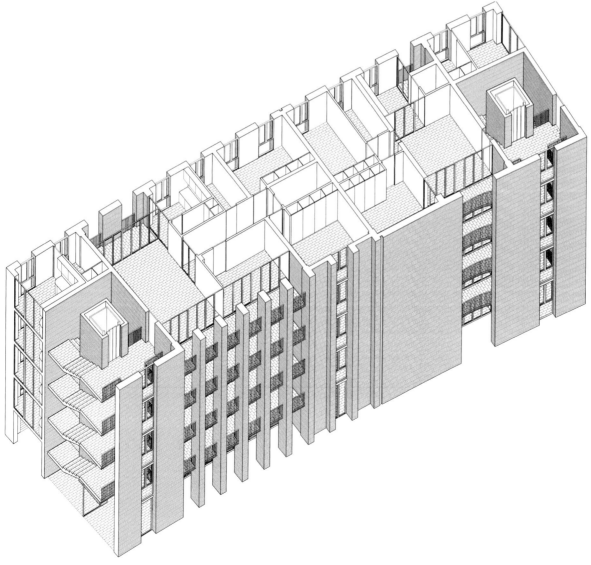

This red brick building has a very clear rhythm of openings and pillars.

The structure of the building is composed of a skeleton of prefabricated concrete elements. The outer walls are of exposed brickwork.

Special attention was paid to eliminating thermal bridges and to acoustic insulation.

The east facade has windows in narrow rows flanked by pillars, whereas the west facade has protected terraces that reproduce the pattern of the windows on the east facade.

All the apartments have views of the exterior and bright interiors. The design of the windows gives rhythm and monumentality to the building, and favours the control of solar gain and temperature in the dwellings.

Two parallel adobe walls contain the dwelling and are extended to delimit the exterior protected spaces: an open-air dining room and a small private garden conceived as an extension of the bedrooms. Traditional local materials such as Civita Castellana adobe, which is porous and irregular, were used. This material, which was already used by the Etruscans, has been adopted for rural construction and is used in this scheme for its expressive nature, its surprising texture and the fact that it compensates for the severity of the straight walls with its calculated lack of precision.

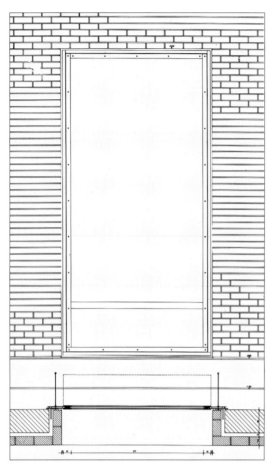

The uniformity of the extensive textured red brickwork facade is interrupted only by the tall steel-profiled Windows. White U-shaped steel profiles are also used to articulate the points of contact with the base in Portuguese granite and the cornice of the building.

Álvaro Siza. Vitra Production Building.

In this house by Botta one can appreciate the adaptability of brickwork for curved walls. Brickwork can be used for straight and curved walls and always offers an image of solidity.

In this case, the red brick is laid in stretcher bonding with a final course of rowlocks.

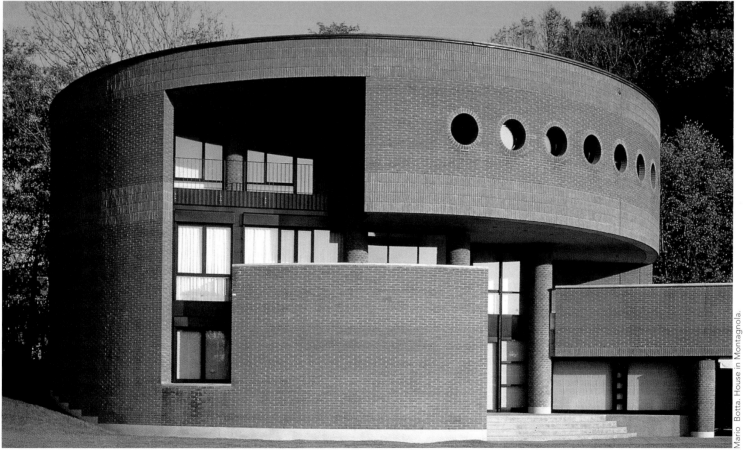

Mario Botta. House in Montagnola.

49

The facade is of red brick with header bonding, and its windows in an irregular combination favour a varied lighting effect in each apartment. The glass facade of the common space provides good communication with the exterior. The panoramic windows face the sun and the inner garden.

The facade of the bedrooms was designed as a glass-clad structure. This window is protected by external shutters that open to offer panoramic views over the canal.

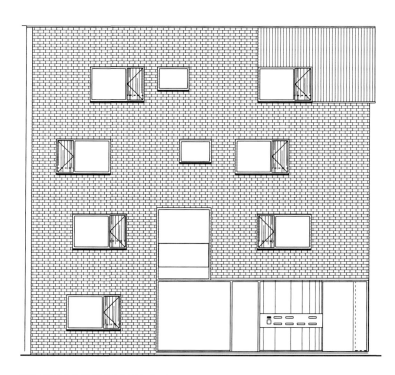

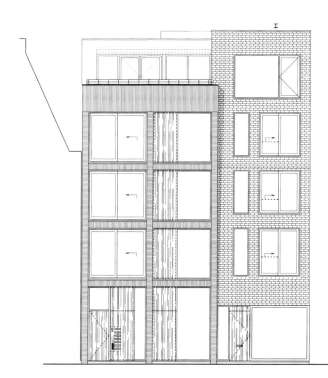

Mecanoo Architecten B.V. Brouwersgracht 280-282 L.A. Rieshuis.

This building is characterized by its rectilinear design and the austere materials used to build it: black fire brick for the facade and basaltic rock for the retaining wall. Urban planning regulations restrict buildings to a single floor, but the sloping site allowed a basement floor to be included as part of the living space.

Traut Architekten. Single Family House.

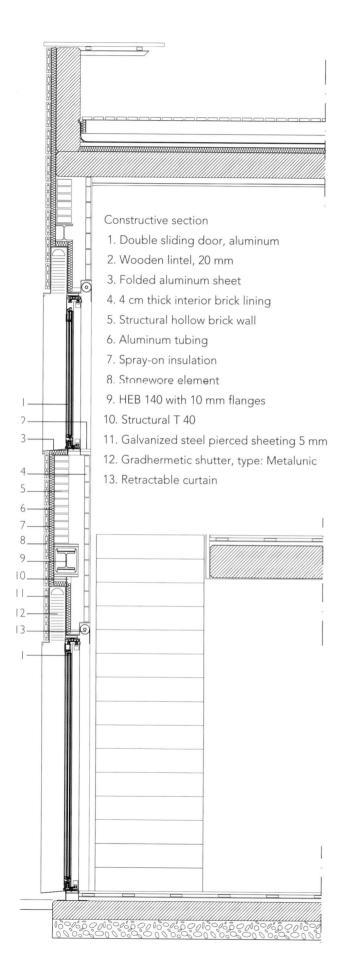

Constructive section

1. Double sliding door, aluminum
2. Wooden lintel, 20 mm
3. Folded aluminum sheet
4. 4 cm thick interior brick lining
5. Structural hollow brick wall
6. Aluminum tubing
7. Spray-on insulation
8. Stoneware element
9. HEB 140 with 10 mm flanges
10. Structural T 40
11. Galvanized steel pierced sheeting 5 mm
12. Gradhermetic shutter, type: Metalunic
13. Retractable curtain

The project was not approached using sophisticated solutions but rather with a sensible use of technology. Even so, there were no special technical details except in the difficulty of execution and in improving the main facades, which were formed by a single plane of solid brick with a lime washed finished on the exterior and plaster on the interior. Once the new openings and voids were adapted, a ventilated façade was designed which contained two layers and the necessary insulation, giving a new exterior image while at the same time ensuring current technology.

To carry this out, the architects custom-designed an earthenware piece supported by stainless steel clamps affixing it to the existing brick. The clamps are hidden, being supported by a series of laterally-placed rods. These clamps can be affixed directly to the wall or, alternately, to vertical fillets wherever there is a need to separate the piece from the wall in order to place sliding panels on some of the balconies.

The doorjambs, ledges and lintels of the openings are 6-millimeter-thick boxes of galvanized sheet metal.

Certain characteristics of the design of the facades influenced the custom-made pieces, which consist of a thin (4 cm) earthenware element with an air chamber cooked at 1200°C. This material was chosen for its structural and visual quality as well as for its inevitable warping, which would distinguish it from the cold perfection of similar cladding materials. The design was approached from a precise laying out of the volumes - a precision which is nonetheless enriched by irregularity.

# VENEER FACADES

The physical separation of the two skins of which a wall is composed, the inner one providing strength and the outer one acting as an envelope, is a fundamental step in the evolution of construction systems. When the outer skin is composed of heavy materials, it is not considered strictly as a veneer facade because the outer skin, generally of stone, concrete or ceramic, transmits the load through a fixing system or a continuous substructure to an inner wall or to the structure of the building; this system has the advantage that the process is reversible. though only partially.

In this type of walls, in addition to gravity, the dynamic action caused by wind or impacts on the lower part of the building must be taken into account. It seldom has a loadbearing function and in general only has to bear its own weight.

The attachment of the veneer marks the composition of the facade: it allows the joints to establish different rhythms in each course through the vertical placing of the elements or their meeting at the joint, since they do not need a lap.

The range of materials that can be used for this type of skin is infinite, though they must fulfil certain requirements: homogeneity and continuity are sought; they must not allow absorption of water by capillary action; and their permeability and durability must also be taken into account.

The material chosen must comply with the mechanical properties of tensile strength and compressive strength; it must also ensure the durability of its initial characteristics after long exposure to sunlight.

The veneer has become a succession of independent elements in terms of mechanical properties and water and air tightness. They are attached at points that allow the panel to behave freely and be totally independent of deformations in the supporting structure.

61

The scheme occupies a site shaped like a ships bow, with majestic curves, each facade presenting a warm and elegant combination of the cladding materials: granite and mirror glass.

The building, whose facade is clad in polished granite panels combined with strips of reflective glass, adapts its sinuous and organic curve to the narrow site on which it is located.

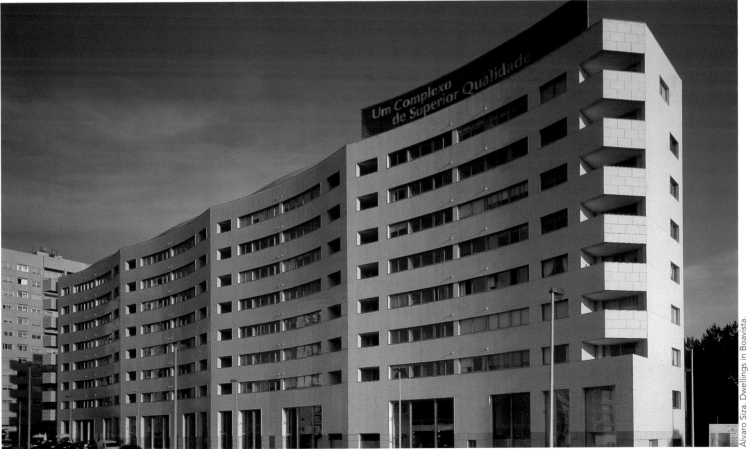

Siza presents the blind facade of the centre as a high granite wall that delimits the enclosure. The external cladding of granite panels, set against the white plaster and marble on the interior, favours the integration in the monumental and holy dimension of the city of Santiago.

The scheme is formed by two large blocks: one that forms the museum with its outbuildings and storage premises, and one that contains the auditorium and the library.

Álvaro Siza. Centro Gallego de Arte Contemporáneo.

This facade has a particular system of blinds with a stainless steel structure and an oxidised copper cladding. The design of this mobile wall emphasises the formal motif of the main facade, which is perforated with long, narrow openings.

The facades are blind, without windows, so the walls seem to be cut by horizontal beams, which cause a striking interplay of light and shade both during the day and at night. The wall is clad in "Santa Fiora" stone. A wide cornice tops the building, casting a large shadow over the facade.

On the other side of the house, a narrow strip between two buildings of different heights, the line of the street is made coherent thanks to a simple rectangular glass facade. A system of stainless steel shutters and panels of oxidised copper completely covers the rear facade and provides the unity of a single plane.

Studio Archea. Housing in Leffe.

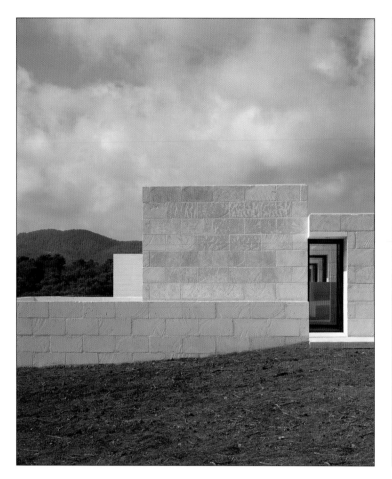

Carlos Ferrater - Joan Guibernau. Tagomago House.

Jordi Guillermo Escriche. Hotel Auditori.

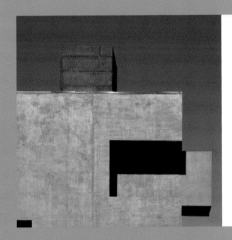

# RENDERED FACADES

Rendered facades can use mortar, plaster, lime, synthetic resins, etc., and manual or mechanical techniques.

The surface to be clad is normally brickwork or concrete. If the wall is of another material it must be primed to improve the adherence of the cladding. The surface is also made rough to improve adherence.

There are the following types:

- Rough cast
- Smooth finish
- Stucco
- Plaster

ROUGH CAST:

According to the application method, rough cast finishes can be divided into:

- **Rendering coat**: applied to brickwork, concrete or rubble when the surface is to be exposed without a high-quality finish or for cladding.

- **Scratch coat/base coat**: applied to surfaces that are to be clad.

SMOOTH FINISH:

According to the finish, these can be divided into:

- **Stone finish**: applied to brickwork, concrete or rubble when a natural stone finish is desired. Also used in walls suffering from damp.

- **Tyrolean rendering**: applied to the same surface as the previous type, but when a rough or rustic finish is required.

STUCCO:

According to the material and the system of application, stucco finishes can be divided into:

- **Trowel applied stucco**: on a base coated with cement mortar, when a uniform finish of medium smoothness is required.

- **Polished stucco**: applied to the same surface as the previous technique when a uniform smooth finish is required.

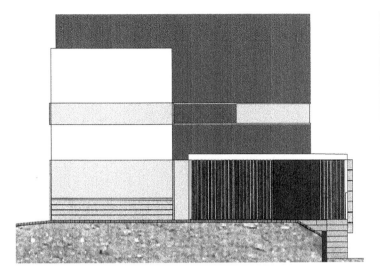

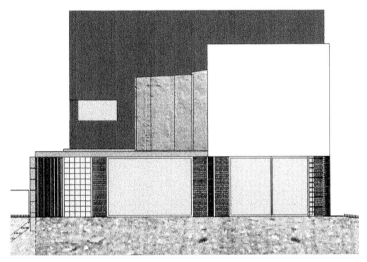

The predominant geometry of the composition is based on cubes of different sizes that present a different face on each side but with a common denominator: the openings, that offer different degrees of contact with the exterior and provide ventilation.

The dwelling is articulated in a series of cubes that lock into each other. The use of different colours and materials on the exterior helps to emphasise the presence of these volumes.

The large sliding glass doors on the ground floor contrast with the appearance of the rest of the building. The structure is a mixed one of reinforced concrete and metal elements. The north and east facades are clad in 25 micron anodised aluminium.

Josep Lluís Mateo & Arturo Vila. House in Artà.

73

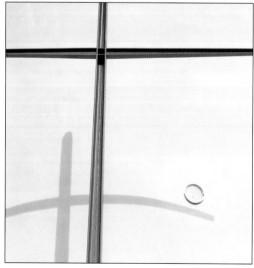

The facade of this church was clad in white render.

In the centre of the curved wall one can see a small circular opening through which a beam of light is cast into the apse. The sunlight enters the church through 25 skylight-domes and many windows situated in the side wall.

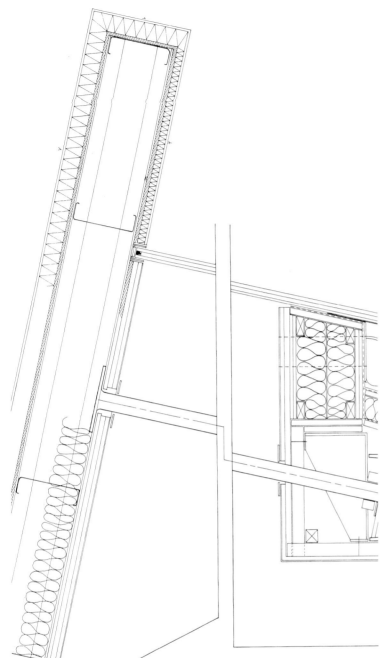

This clinic was designed with a thick, reflective form to shield its occupants from the noise and pollution generated by the nearby roundabout and flyover. The fluid form of the building is like a gentle white skin with a double curve, composed of panels that provide new architectural qualities and brightness to a zone dominated by the strong linear character of the roads that run through it. The facade is broken up into curved overlapping panels with a free space between them that frames the views toward the exterior. The exterior finish consists of a rough coat of acrylic STO 6 mm on small insulating panels. The structure is of 50 mm cold galvanised angular profile.

Guy Greenfield. Docctors-Surgery in West London.

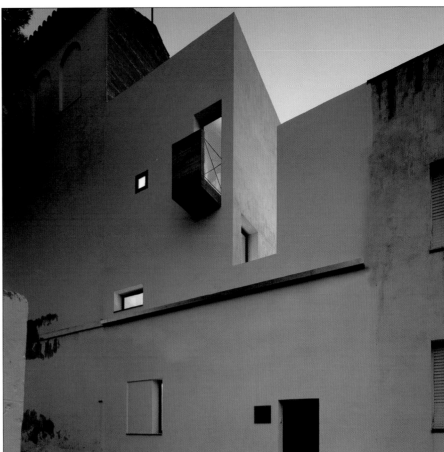

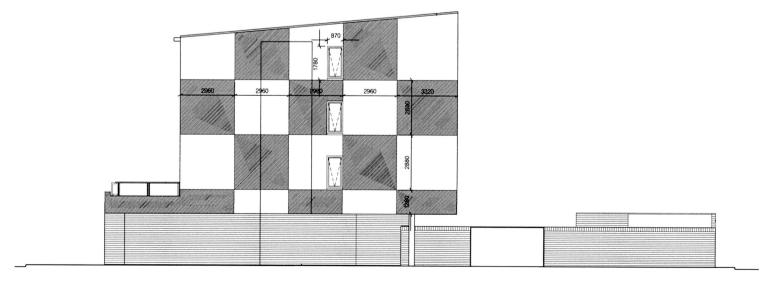

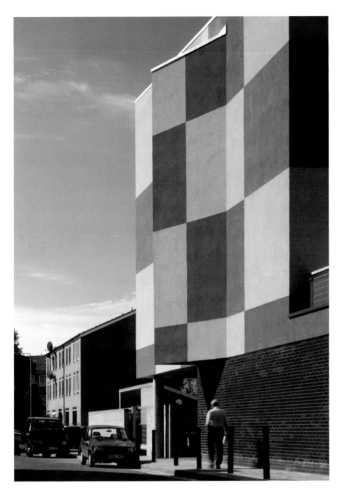

For the treatment of the facade, the architects did not attempt to imitate the buildings of the zone. The facade was adorned with a chequered motif of light blue and grey, creating a surprising effect of camouflaged architecture. The chequered pattern extends to the south facade, where panels of transparent and translucent glass alternate, and mitigate the effect of a totally uniform glazed surface.

This scheme proposes a longitudinal layout of parallel wings perforated by many openings toward the courts and gardens.
The treatment of the outer walls, rendered in cement oxidised with ferrous sulphate, shows the architects' wish to integrate the volumes of the building into an environment of reddish earth.
The complex, understood as a single space, fits in with the colours of the earth and the surrounding vegetation.
The openings in the walls emphasise their thickness.
The black painted aluminium frames contrast with the finish of the exterior walls.

Ignacio Vicens & Jose Antonio Ramos. Residence for elderly.

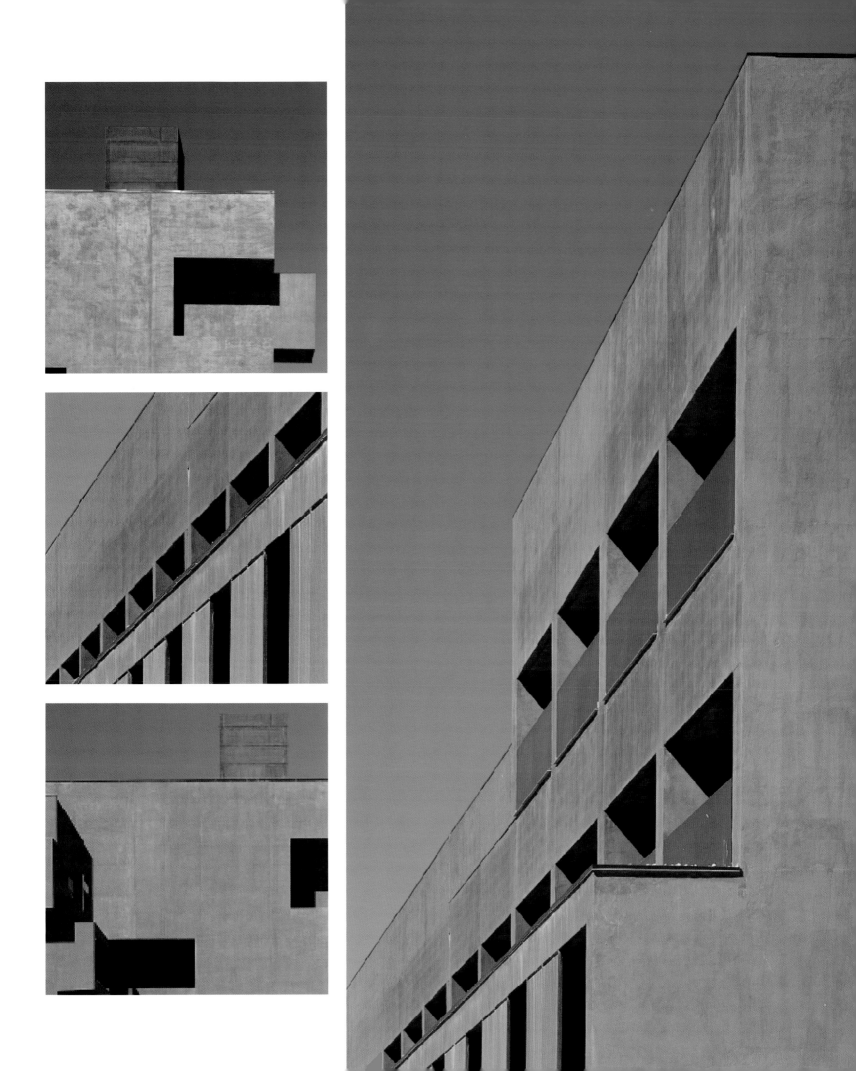

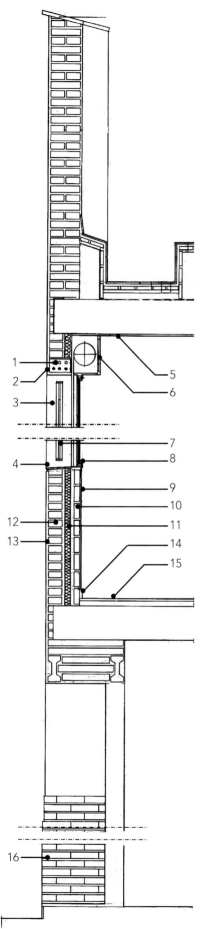

Window lintel:

1. Reinforced header vertical bricks
2. Exterior side rendering coat
3. Interior side rendering coat
4. Windowsill configured by 14x28cm ceramic tile aligned with parapet
5. Three coat plaster and plaster dressing
6. Blinds box with interior register
7. Galvanized steel profile joinery
8. Grating (first two floors)
9. Plaster finish and reinforcement
10. Air brick partition wall, e=4cm
11. Projected polyurethane, e=3cm
12. Airbrick zither, e=9cm
13. Rendering coat
14. White terrazzo stripe baseboard, e=7cm
15. White terrazzo, 33x33cm
16. Vitreous stretcher and header air bricks

José Ramón Sierra Delgado. Housing in Polígono Aeropuerto.

pool Architektur. In spe-single family house.

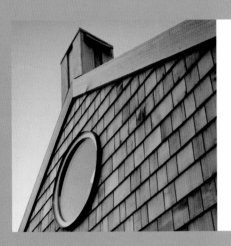

# WOODEN FACADES

Though wood is a material that has been used constantly throughout history, wooden facades have never been very common. Buildings with a wooden structure normally have rubble facades.

At present, we find buildings in which wood is used very rationally on the facade by applying new technologies and knowledge to take full advantage of this material.

Though wooden walls have good thermal properties, an inner layer is normally added to improve the insulation. Also, thanks to mechanisation and industrialisation in the treatment of wood, the joints and fits of the pieces are far more precise, thus ensuring better protection from rain and wind. Furthermore, the wood is treated with additives to provide protection from insects and fire, which give it greater durability and strength. Wooden elements made from chips and layers processed in the factory also offer better strength and weather resistance.

There are several types of loadbearing timber facades. The traditional Finnish system, for example uses logs that lock together at the corners, forming the final finish. Another system is the balloon-frame. This is a lighter construction than the Finnish system, using small-section uprights that support cross-members that support the beams and joists of the frame of the building. The exterior finish is of tongue and groove boards.

Exterior cladding of wood tends to consist of high-density panels or slats treated with additives to provide protection against moisture, fire and insects. There are currently a great variety of products on the market, with different thicknesses and finishes. One must bear in mind the need to protect the edges of the wood panels.

This system of facade elements is pre-fabricated and composed of an exterior cladding of oak, with rock wool insulation and some of the services incorporated in its interior. Each of these elements forms a disposable formwork into which the concrete is poured, and it thus has a structural function, as well as providing acoustic insulation and fire protection.

The wood is proposed as an element of identity in an environment where this material is not common, and at the same time as an attempt to incorporate some traditional construction solutions of the Tyrol.

The dialogue with the exterior is achieved through a sequence of balconies that stand out from the south facade like transparent boxes. Doors make these spaces independent from the rest of the dwelling, and full-height sliding panels open them completely to the exterior.

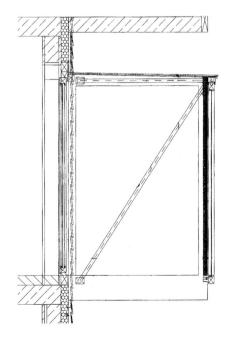

This two-storey house built in oak wood houses the workshop and dwelling of an artist.

One of the most striking features of the scheme is the arrangement of a series of sliding panels of the same wood that when closed convert the house into a blind, hermetic box.

When the panels are opened, the users enjoy a balcony that surrounds the dwelling, and when they are closed they have extra space for the rooms.

The open joints of the external wood cladding create horizontal strips of sunlight when the panels are closed. When the panels are open there is a fluid relation between the interior and the exterior.

Hiroshi Naito. House and Studio for an Artist.

The villa is clad in oak slats in a system of varying thickness, which visually plays with the facetted patination of the wooden slats. It is thus a house which, in its visual and textual appearance, will continue for many years to come to undergo a process of change towards a more permanent form of expression.

C. F. Møller Architects. Villa Råhøj Allé.

# CEDAR FACADES

This bright, compact dwelling is located on an embankment and was made in cedar wood. The ground plan and elevations are determined by the good views to the south, and also by the neighbouring buildings to the north, which limit the views. Whereas both the north-facing main access and the side windows only offer partial views, the southern face of the dwelling opens onto the surrounding nature through a large glazed surface.

Morger & Degelo Architekten. Nadolny House.

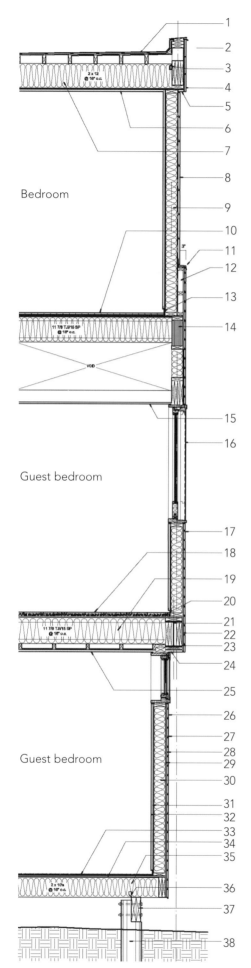

Bedroom

Guest bedroom

Guest bedroom

Wall section at guest bedroom

1. Fiberglass roof over ¾'' exterior grade plywood slope to drain
2. Lead coated copper parapet (typical)
3. Hurricane clips at each joist (typical)
4. 1 x 10 rabbeted cedar fascia
5. Cedar soffit over ¾'' exterior grade plywood
6. Veneer plaster sheetrock
7. Insulation: R30 Kraft face, fiberglass batts
8. 12'' Shiplap cedar siding recessed between windows
9. Insulation: R19 Kraft face, fiberglass batts
10. 3'' T&G ebonized oak flooring
11. Lead coated copper flashing
12. 3'' furr-out over recessed shear wall with 4'' Shiplap cedar siding
13. 2 ½ Fry reglet reveal base
14. 5 ¼x117/8'' P.L.
15. Veneer plaster sheetrock
16. 2 x 6 shear wall beyond
17. 2 x 6 shear wall with 4'' Shiplap cedar siding
18. ¾'' Stone floor over 1'' setting bed and ¾'' plywood subfloor
19. Insulation: R22 Kraft face, fiberglass batts
20. 2 ½ Fry reglet reveal base
21. Steel structure
22. Vapor barrier
23. Exterior grade plywood
24. T&G Cedar soffit over ½'' exterior grade plywood
25. Veneer plaster sheetrock over ½'' plywood
26. 2x6 shear wall with ½'' plywood each side
27. 4'' Shiplap cedar siding
28. Vapor barrier
29. ½'' exterior grade plywood
30. Insulation: R19 Kraft face, fiberglass batts
31. ½'' plywood
32. Veneer plaster sheetrock
33. Carpet & underlayment
34. ¾'' plywood
35. Insulation: R22 Kraft face, fiberglass batts
36. Hurricane clips at each joist (typical)
37. (2) 3x12' s (typical)
38. 12'' typical pile

Christoff Finio. Beach House.

92

The walls and the roof are covered by shingles made of Canadian Cedar. The wood is left untreated, and will adapt to the colours of the rocks.

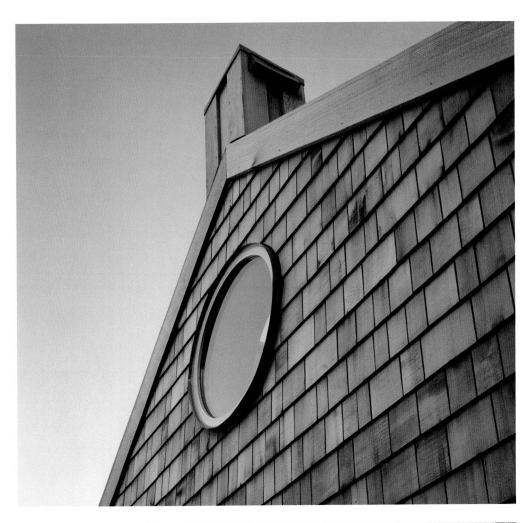

Wingårdh Arkitektkontor AB. Villa Tjuvkil.

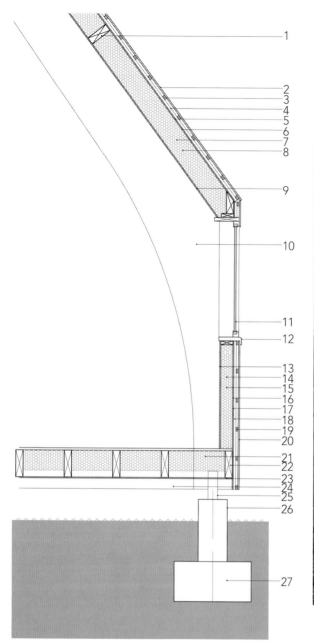

Detail of windows facing east and west

1. Roof beam 75x25

2. Red cedar roof-shingles

3. Horizontal lathing 25x38

4. Vertical counterlathing 25x38

5. Panel Oriented Strand Board 10 mm

6. Waterproofing layer

7. Rockwool

8. Beams of Norway Pine

9. Panels of pinewood ply10 mm

10. Enclosure of laminated glued Norway pine

11. Double-glazing 4/12/6

12. Carpentry of local pinewood, varnished interior, scorched exterior

13. Panels of pinewood ply10 mm

14. Risers of Norway pine 38x125

15. Rockwool

16. Panel Oriented Strand Board 10 mm

17. Waterproofing layer

18. Vertical counterlathing 38x25

19. Horizontal lathing 38x25

20. Red cedar roof-shingles

21. Rockwool

22. Joists of laminated wood, glued 90x360

23. Lower side: OSB 10 mm

24. Baseplate of glued laminated wood 90x360

25. Steel fixtures

26. Concrete pile

27. Frost-proof concrete foundation shoe, 600x600x400

The exterior is clad with red cedar shingles; it changes under varying weather conditions, orange and shining in the rain, silvery in the sun

Jean-Baptiste Barache. House in Normandie.

Dietricht Fink & Thomas Jocher. Two multifamily Dwellings.

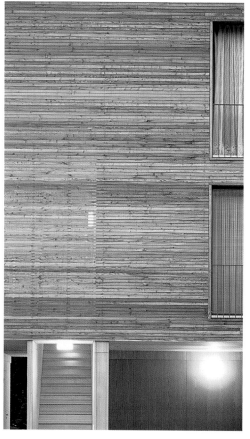

The building was constructed with wood frames and mainly prefabricated elements, which reduced construction time to four months.

The aesthetics are determined by the use of a small selection of materials, each one used with its natural surface texture. In order to emulate the proportion of openings and walls of old dwellings of historic interest, an external skin of narrow larch wood slats was designed to conceal the open stairs, so that they are not visible from the exterior.

The light filters through this skin toward the stairs during the day, whereas at night the artificial lighting articulates the openings on the facade and provides lighting in the court. Large panels of smooth plywood were used only where the cubes are incised, in the areas of direct contact between the building and its inhabitants.

The exterior wall does not have a homogenous surface, but is broken by the effect of light and shade and by the filter of larch wood boards.

This is a clear example in which the envelope of the building is formed by slats of wood, with a wide separation between them, as one normally imagines an element formed by slats.

Augustin & Frank. Viesel House.

The whole structure is lined inside and outside with layers of insulation, waterproofing and a cladding of wood. The wood used is untreated larch with vertical joints into which metal channels fit that facilitate drainage.

One of the solutions for economy and speed was to reduce the number of windows and limit them to two types: normal windows of 1.20 m height and glazed doors on the ground floor. With larch wood frames, the openings of the south facade form a continuous sequence of windows on the first floor and of doors on the ground floor, following a traditional pattern of domestic architecture in the area.

The self-supporting facades were made with panels of untreated larch that, with the passing of time, acquire a silvery grey patina that will provide weather protection.

The only building process carried out in situ was the construction of the reinforced concrete basement. The rest of the assembly was performed with prefabricated wood elements, which reduce costs and facilitate the construction process.

Marco Koeppel & Carlos Martinez. Siedlung Prosa.

A very unusual solution for the facade in terms of cubic architecture: a cladding of larch siding. In this region this is a traditional material that has proven its value and lasting quality in the difficult climatic conditions that are found at this altitude. An interesting feature is the volumetric relation of the greenhouses or loggias that stand out from the south facades, and the arrangement of the windows and the stairs in the access areas, which give the buildings a random appearance that is less severe than that of conventional apartment blocks. The skin of wood scales, a regional sign of identity and a local building resource, is recovered like a tailor-made suit. The cladding of wood tiles takes on new connotations.

Carlo Baumschlager & Dietmar Eberle. Multi-storey housing in Nüzinders.

As in the entire project, the large windows are prototypes, which operate with a remarkably simple wheel mechanism. Sliding frames with mosquito netting discourage undesirable guests. The "Tall House" has two extra windows, one overlooking the lake, another facing the stars.

UdK Berlin. Project 1:1 Valentinswerder.

The locally sourced timber cladding in alternating strips of smooth sawn larch and rough sawn douglas fir contrasts with the minimalist interior with its bespoke furniture and suggests the conjunction of the temporal and the transcendent to which the retreat tradition is devoted.

Architects Bates Maher. Glencomeargh House.

The 285 sqm floor area is divided into two parallelepiped elements, with one set back slightly from the other.

Parallel walls clad in pressed wood panels are used for the interior divisions of the dwelling, defining spaces that are closed by windows on the north and south sides.

Kramer E. Woodard. Highbridge - The Yanni Residence.

Render and copper cladding mark the zones of the penthouse. The large panels of laminated wood on the facade were impregnated to provide fire protection and dyed a red-orange colour.

The windows were placed in the same plane as the facade of wood and render, so the outer skin forms a flat, precise surface.

The front volume, with its ground floor completely glazed, is clad with boards of red spruce in vertical strips. Thus, as there are no horizontal joints, deterioration due to moisture is avoided.

Alsop & Stormer. Theresienstieg Herbert-Weichmann-Strasse.

The apartments are accessed from the common space along the north facade. The cladding of the south facade, of red and orange painted wood, marks a contrast with the surrounding vegetation and with the concrete wall that closes the building to the north.

Splitterwerk. Complex Red Tree Frog.

The main material used for the construction was wood: on the exterior all the wood cladding was dyed white. Within the general rigour, the only ornamental licence of the scheme was the vertical placing of the boards in the smaller volume, whereas in the larger volume they are placed horizontally, emphasising the functional independence of each block.

Mathias Klotz. Ugarte House.

The exterior cladding consists of three-layered Douglas-fir plywood, rough-finished, treated with a protective varnish over a base-coat of natural oils. The walls of the ground-floor are made of wood with exterior shelving to contain the firewood. The walls of the upper floor are double layered wood planking with an aerated insulation layer inside.

Hemmi Fayet Architekten. Vacation House at Zinal.

The warm redwood timber contrasts with stainless steel details in these two houses built on a subdivided corner block. Irregularly shaped windows frame the surrounding environment, including a cathedral on the opposite corner.

MS-31 STUDIO. State & Date.

The floors, walls and ceilings of the large living space and the bedrooms are all clad in the same wooden boarding. All the exterior surface area is surfaced by rough-sawn pine boards and vertical joint covers with a black finish of charcoal oil, often used on the local rural constructions.

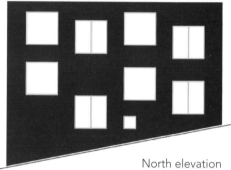

North elevation

Pezo von Ellrichshausen Arquitectos. Rivo House.

Entirely built of local Australian hardwood timbers and glass, the house combines one of the oldest building materials with a modern form, the cube. The solid timber doors and windows are integrated into the timber walls, to make the form, externally, as sheer as possible.

Nicholas Murcutt. Box House.

109

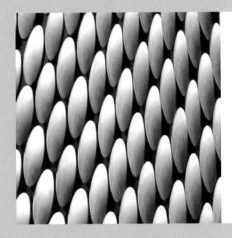

# METAL FACADES

Metal claddings offer many possibilities for the exterior finish of a facade. On the market one can find panels of several types of metal. The materials most used are aluminium and galvanised steel, though one can also find panels of stainless steel, copper and zinc.

Metal panels can be of two types: single-layer or multi-layer panels.

Single-layer panels have the advantage of being very light, not absorbing water and in cases of fire they do not give off toxic gases, though they involve problems of condensation and thermal expansion. To solve the problem of condensation, ventilated facades are used. The problem of thermal expansion means that the structures must be able to absorb the increase in size. Small-size panels, some of greater thickness, with a greater number of joints are therefore used. Geometric solutions allowing the free movement of the panels are also used, such as folds at the edges of the panels.

Multi-layer panels formed by two sheets with a jointing material between them offer greater resistance to deformation. According to the type of jointing material, the panels may be thermally inert or insulating. Inert panels using materials such as polyethylene offer greater strength and absorb expansion without the need to increase the thickness of the metal plate, so panels of considerable size can be used (up to 8 metres long by 1.5 m wide). Furthermore, as there is no thermal insulation between the two metal sheets, there is no problem of thermal expansion between the two. In general the facades are ventilated to avoid condensation.

In insulating panels the jointing material is a thermal insulation of mineral wool, polyurethane or polycyanurate. This solution avoids condensation and increases the resistance of the panel to deformation. However, there is a problem of differential expansion between the two faces of the panel, which can lead to curvature and deformation, so it is preferable to use small panels. As the insulation is in the panel itself, one must maintain the two layers constantly isolated, even at the edges, to avoid a thermal bridge.

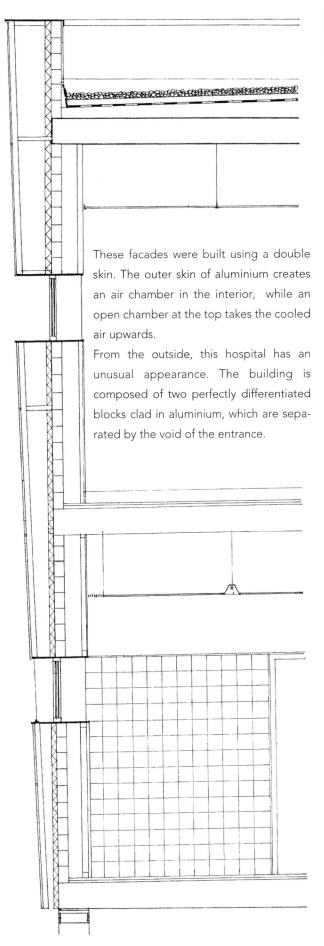

These facades were built using a double skin. The outer skin of aluminium creates an air chamber in the interior, while an open chamber at the top takes the cooled air upwards.

From the outside, this hospital has an unusual appearance. The building is composed of two perfectly differentiated blocks clad in aluminium, which are separated by the void of the entrance.

Arnaldo Basadonna. Centre d'Atenció Primaria.

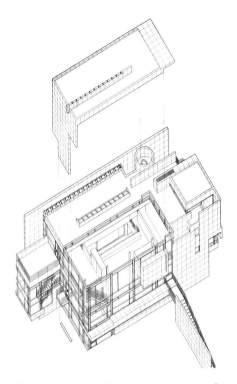

This private residence-museum stands on a black granite podium that extends outwards at the front and rear of the main volume. The white volume of the house, which stands on pilotis, floats above the podium like an opaque plane, perforated by several openings.

The front facade, clad in metal, protects the dwelling areas, whereas the north and west facades have curtain walls that, together with the opaque main facade, direct the interior space toward a small pool in the southwest area.

The exterior of the house is clad in panels of white painted aluminium with aluminium-framed, insulating windows.

Richard Meier. Rachofksy House.

115

On this page, the building materials are pre-fabricated: large panels for light buildings supported by pillars mounted on the foundations and trapezoidal rough aluminium sheet on the surfaces of the facades. The wooden elements were simply treated with wax.

North side: the facade is practically blind, because of the nearby railway.

On the following page, the facades of the prismatic volumes are resolved through large planes of aluminium panels, strategically cut by horizontal glazed strips. Another feature is the vertical glazing that houses the stairwell on the west facade.

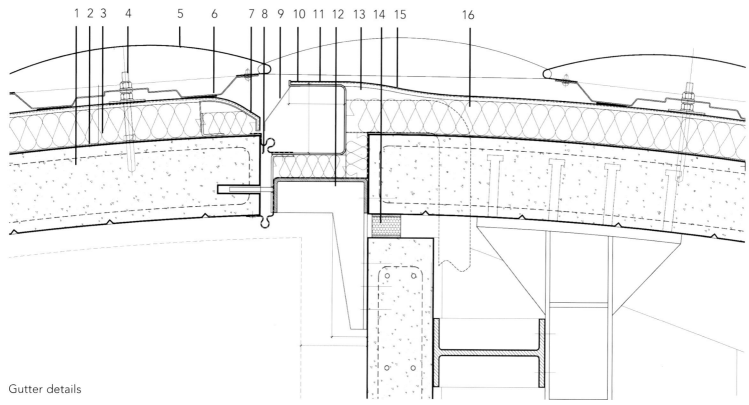

Gutter details

1. 175 mm sprayed concrete panel
2. Liquid applied membrane
3. 75 mm insulation
4. Stainless steel under reamed expanding anchor

5. Natural anodised aluminium disk
6. Black anodised aluminium support ring
7. Continuous render stop end
8. Horizontal movement joint

9. Aluminium mesh screen
10. Liquid applied membrane
11. Gutter made from pressed aluminum with continuous heat-welded membrane
12. Continuous steel C section

designed by OAP to restrain base of upper panel
13. Profiled insulation
14. Fire stop
15. Liquid applied membrane
16. 75 mm insulation

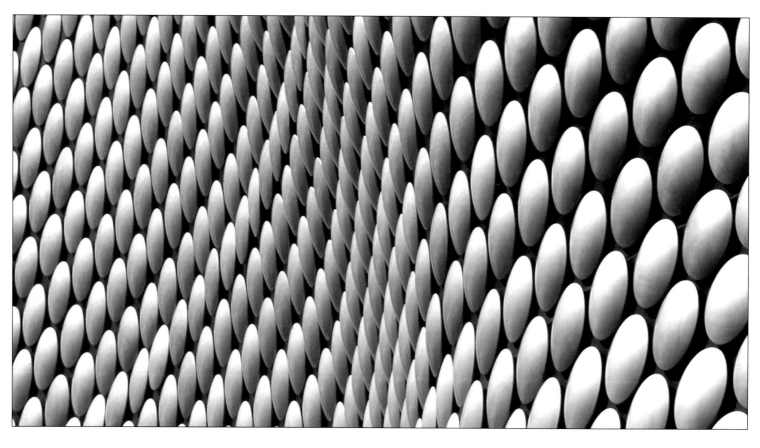

1. Corner moldings, powder-coated aluminum.

2. Lintel moldings around the windows, powder-coated aluminum

3. Powder coated radial cut aluminum siding along the façade

4. Lintel moldings, powder-coated aluminum

5. Multi-layered plexiglas glazing sheets, translucent white, 8 mm cold pierced

6. Zincified steel angle irons, approx. 80x60 mm, curved to façade radius.
   Inner radius: 4940 mm
   Outer radius: 5020 mm

7. UK Steel stand, zincified, with slot.

8. Sims six-layer powder-coated aluminum sheeting, sanded

9. Façade insulation system and translucent roofing

10. Composition flooring for heatstorage

11. Deck, new

12. Structural steel beam

13. Roof components

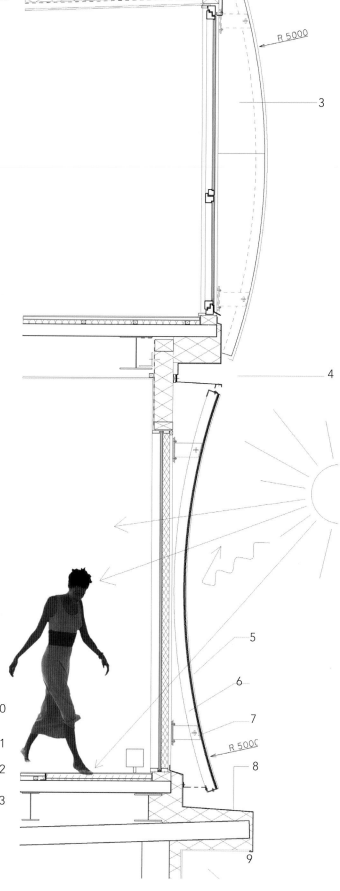

Spine2.Schanzenupgrade.

Antoine Pedrock. American Heritage Center and Art Museum.

The copper cone located in the centre of the building corresponds to a nearby circular basketball stadium, but also recalls the images of unidentified flying objects, a volcano or a warrior's shield.

This scheme is constructed basically in granulated reinforced concrete blocks that form simple and forceful geometric compositions.

It is a cube of six levels, built in concrete and clad in 20 cm thick copper panels. In some zones the arrangement of the panels allows sunlight through. The copper cladding conceals the number of levels and the structure of the building. The arrangement of the copper panels creates optical effects on the surfaces of the cube, which reinforce the image of mysterious sobriety and calm ambiguity. The volume modifies its exterior appearance as the copper is oxidised and changes its colour and texture.

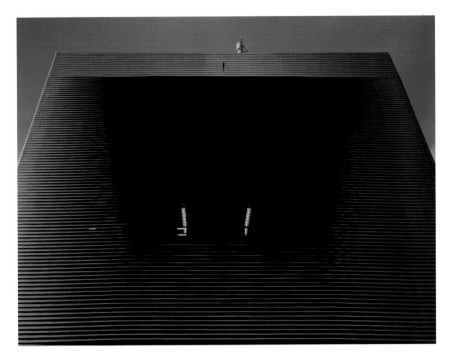

Jacques Herzog & Pierre de Meuron. Signal Box auf dem Wolf.

123

The transparent glazed ground floor is complemented by the copper facade of the floor above. The red copper panels are arranged to form a pattern in relief, with a play of lights. In time the red from the copper will turn to dark brown and finish up as a green patina, the permanent, oxidized layer that protects the material.

Aldo Celoria. Travella House.

This building, clad in copper with a gold finish, was built on a narrow trapezoidal site. The construction presents an excellent design with impressive solutions for the details.

# CORTEN STEEL FACADES

This scheme is materialised in a compact container of 60 metres of facade.

The main facade has a double identity, of day and night. During the day, it is a blind wall covered with a skin of oxidised corten steel, with a narrow opening for the en-trance, and access through a glass bridge that runs over a narrow ditch. With the exception of these two doors, the facade appears impenetrable. These openings are protected by a glass canopy.

At night everything changes, and the facade is transformed into a wall perforated by tiny points of light that reflect the interior light and dematerialise the steel panels.

Studio Archea. Stop Line Disco-Bar.

126

The exterior of the dwelling is clad in panels of corten steel, which will darken as a result of erosion, changing from black to bright red with the passing of time.

Hiroshi Nakao. House with Studio for a Flower Artist.

The clearly differentiated parts of the building are juxtaposed simultaneously rather than chaotically. Different construction systems, the old and the new, coexist and interrelate. The design of the facade, with partially mobile panels of zinc-coated metal mesh, creates spaces of transition and interstices.

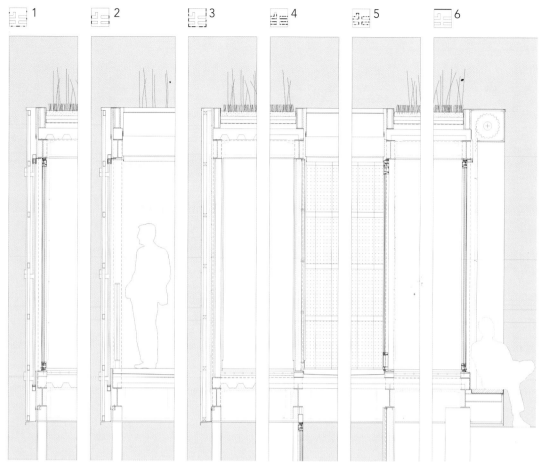

1. Section of zinc shutters
2. Section of zinc shutters in courtyard
3. Section of zinc facade
4. Section of shutters in courtyard
5. Section of voids in courtyard
6. Section of north facade

131

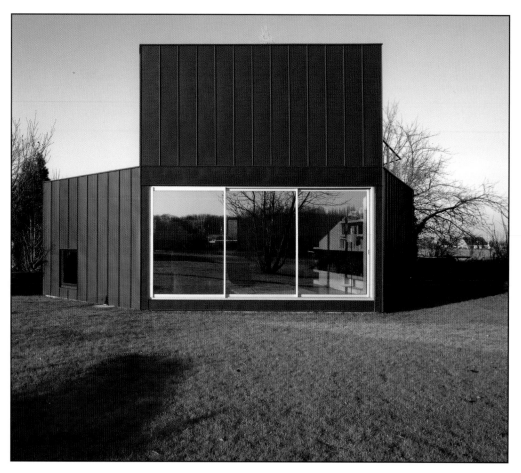

The façades have been entirely clad in an unusual material, anthracite zinc, which is animated by the various ways it is used and the play of light on the building's different facets. The folds in the cladding are oriented vertically and the installation has been carried out with the greatest care, a reference to the craftsmanship of the region.

Tank Architectes. Black House.

132

The skin of the building is characterized by very refined detailing across the complex geometry. The detailing and geometry applied does not only control the physical and structural characteristics, but also especially the aesthetics of the building. The use of natural materials (concrete, steel, aluminum, black zinc, wood) supports the timeless and monolithical character of the building.

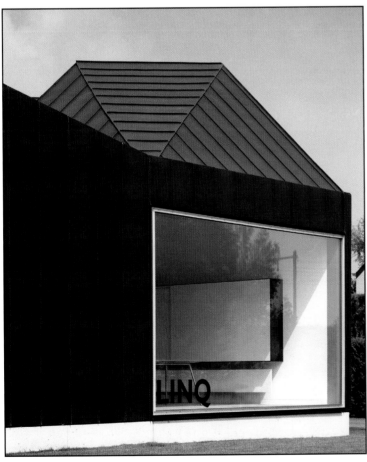

NU architectuuratelier. Bureaux-Habitation, Gand.

133

At first glance, the Cell Brick House seems to be a structure of piled-up concrete blocks, but on closer inspection one sees that these blocks are in fact steel boxes.

Atelier Tekuto. Cell Brick House.

The 80 metre entrance facade is transformed into an intelligent image of innovative architectural solutions. A structure with a double layer of perforated metal, situated in front of the black frame of the building, produces a striking effect thanks to the use of neon lights. The small black orifices are transformed into mobile strips that accompany the observers along their journey, or guide them to a perspective of endless depth as they approach. The grey aluminium links the interior and the exterior to form a whole.

The skin of the building is formed by a double layer of perforated metal plate. The neon lighting system in the interior produces a great visual impact.

Gorgona Boehm Associates. Supermarket Merkur.

136

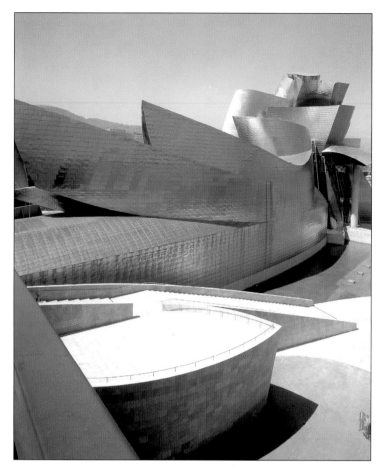

Frank O. Gehry & Associates. Museum Guggenheim Bilbao.

RCR - Rafael Aranda, Carme Pigem, Ramón Vilalta, Arquitectes. M-Lidia House.

139

# GLASS FACADES

Throughout history the search for slim, light walls that are self-supporting, and offer weather protection and acoustic and thermal insulation has led to the use of glass as the material that is able to overcome the antithesis between interior and exterior. The building of skin and bones only became possible when industry learned how to make stratified glass providing a perfect weather seal and efficient air-conditioning systems.

Transparency is the key to the appearance of modern architecture. The openings can be far larger thanks to the possibilities offered by the new glass techniques, but this increase in size must be combined with an analysis of the consequences for the interior environment.

In order to design a suitable protection from sunlight, certain limitations must be taken into account. The need for solar gain in winter, the requirement of clear direct views of the exterior, and the logical desire to achieve the maximum level of interior lightning are the three most difficult conditions to combine, through the use of louvers, stained glass and other forms of solar protection. However, the disadvantages of completely glazed buildings are obvious: loss of heat in winter and overheating in summer.

There are many interesting solutions for facades of buildings that are environment friendly. This approach considerably reduces energy losses in winter and overheating in summer. The range of possibilities and combinations may be divided into the following categories:

- **Single-layer facades**, elements of solar protection, exterior or interior; or with these elements incorporated in the empty space between window panes.

- **Multi-layer facades**, such as ventilated or double layer facades.

Single layer facades are based on glazing and added control elements. An exterior control element is more efficient than an interior one, because if the element is on the outside it keeps the excess heat from entering the building. However, the effects of the atmospheric conditions can greatly increase the costs of cleaning and maintenance.

A multi-layer facade is created by adding a simple pane of glass, either in front of or behind the existing layer of double glazing. The empty space is connected to both the interior and the exterior air. Solar control devices are placed between the layers of glass to protect them from the weather. Mechanical ventilation provides the necessary air flow.

This construction, based on a three-dimensional grid, adopts the form of a glass box of 6 x 15 x 12 metres. The building is divided vertically into four parts. The office, located on the top level, occupies the two higher volumes, whereas the two lower floors house the dwelling.

The building is wrapped in a thin skin of transparent glass, which embraces the four facades and helps to convert the interior into a clear, bright space during the day.

The four facades of transparent glass can increase their degree of privacy and protection from sunlight through the use of mobile insulating curtains.

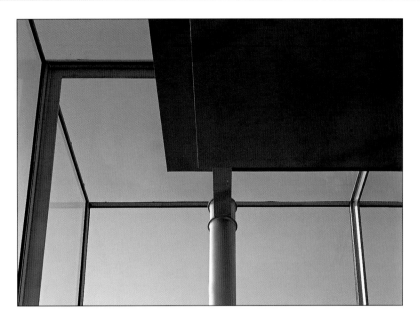

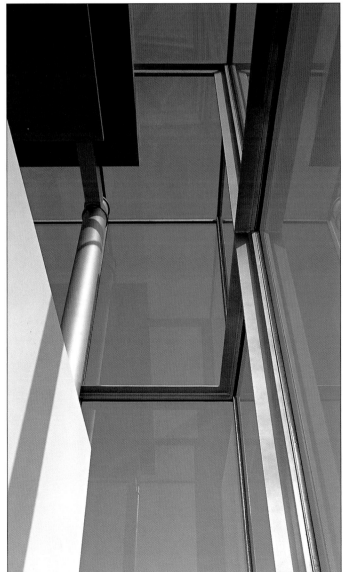

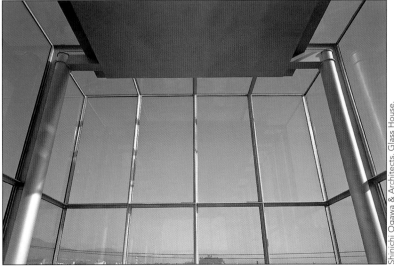

Shinichi Ogawa & Architects. Glass House.

The continuity is ensured through a careful selection of materials (glass, aluminium and steel) and colours (white, grey and silver). The walls are built with glass, sometimes transparent and sometimes covered with a great variety of densities of ceramic to ensure a suitable level of transparency and definition of the surfaces. The transparency of the glass ensures the visual continuity between the access area, the hall and the terrace of the garden.

With four L-shaped towers like open books facing each other and delimiting a symbolic space, the library imposes its presence and has a clear identity.

The aim of the architect was to clad the building in panels of glass that were as large and transparent as possible.

The towers were clad in the most transparent glass available in order to accentuate their immaterial nature.

Dominique Perrault. Bibliothèque Nationale.

Renzo Piano Building Workshop. P&C Department Store.

147

# TRANSLUCENT GLASS FACADES

Florian Nagler Architekten. Factory Hall.

Behind its shell of frosted glass, enclosing a space of approximately 2500 sqm, the building's former shape has achieved a new identity. Night transforms the building into a checkered lantern, the pattern constantly altered by its inhabitants. Details of the old façade can be guessed through the translucent new shell.

The light-soaked corridors that are sandwiched between the new outer skin and the old wall provide acoustic and thermal insulation. The privacy behind the frosted glass shell is only pierced by chosen perspectives of the environment outside; these transparent strips are the only ornament that interrupts the sheer surface.

Taller de Enrique Norten Arquitectos, SC (TEN Arquitectos). Hotel Habita.

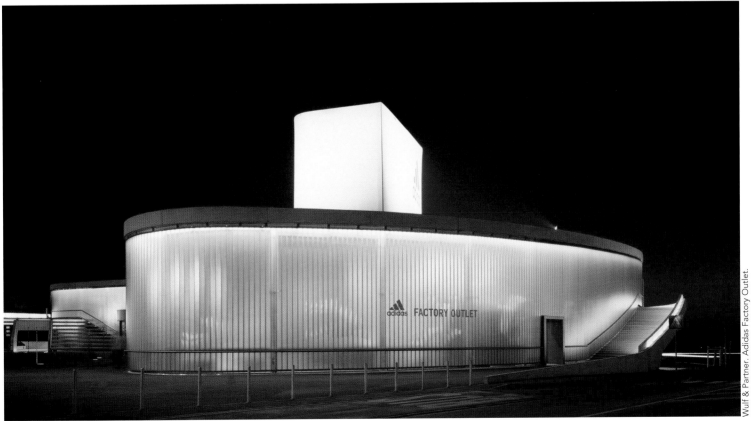

Wulf & Partner. Adidas Factory Outlet.

# SCREENPRINTED GLASS FACADES

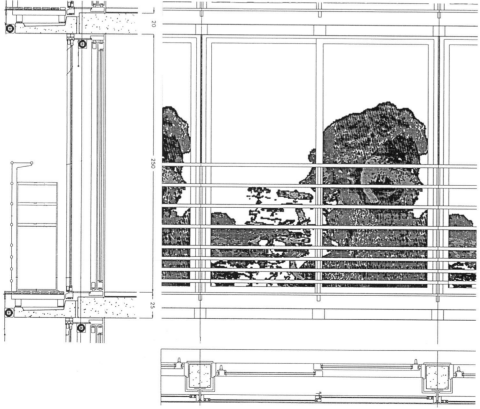

This apartment building is an elegant and discreet complex that stands out because of the decorative freedom applied by the architect on the window panes of all the apartments.

In the design of the facade, the idea was to provide floor-to-ceiling glazing in each apartment, with sliding doors to avoid loss of space. The exterior joinery is of varnished black aluminium and the interior joinery of the double-glazed windows is of wood.

The coloured enamelled images are printed on the outer skin of glass.

The motifs used to cover the glass facade are scenes from the frescos by Giulio Romano in the Palazzo del Té in Mantua. The use of such bright colours creates a succession of clearly defined wall images.

This is a building with a compact volumetric configuration in order to preserve the local vegetation as far as possible. With its vegetation-covered roof and its screen-printed facade, the building attempts to restore the spatial order of the park.

The centre is formed by a plinth with a mineral appearance made of reinforced concrete, which houses the main restaurant, and a fully-glazed volume with a metal structure that houses the rehabilitation facility. These two elements are surrounded and unified by a screen-printed glass skin with a plant motif. The windows of the terrace, screen-printed with vegetable motifs, give privacy and coolness, and acoustic insulation from the exterior.

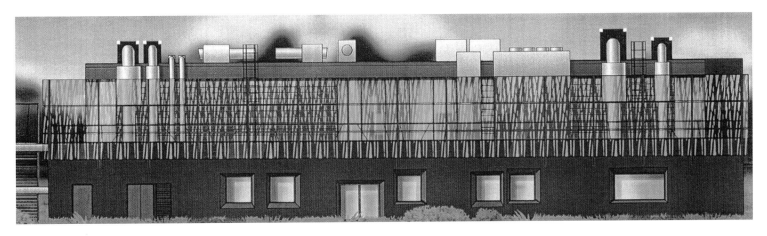

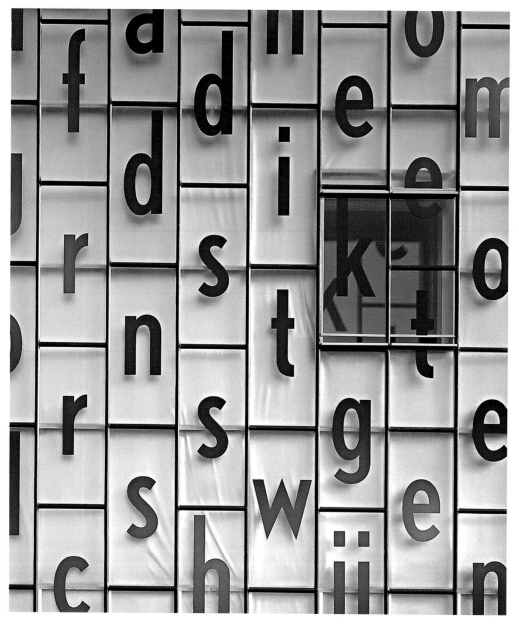

To avoid the traditional separation between workers and management, it was decided to build a false facade to wrap the building. The facade is composed of three sections: a black plinth of concrete, a row of windows that open in the plinth and, above, a glazed section formed by panels of decorated glass, mounted on a simple framework similar to that used to build greenhouses. The volume is broken at two points: the main access, where the logotype of the company acts as a pillar, and the access to the offices.

The facade with its letters suggests the nature of the company. In the glass a text by the Dutch poet K. Schippers was engraved, with a typography in bold face designed by K. Martens.

157

The project collated and organized the different existing types of architecture, like sedimentation that bears witness to each period. The reference material was glass, transparent or white, translucent or colored, and Mondrian's pictorial language - the geometry of the absolute - was used as a design reference.

Dominique Perrault. Town Hall / Hybrid Hotel.

The cladding, designed by Prof. Thomas Bayrle of the Frankfurt school of fine arts, consists of over 550 sheets of glass with silk screened motifs of fractal patterns, using images related to the city of Kassel. Curved sheets were used for the rounded corners, so the surface reads like single membrane shimmering over the white concrete wall. Varying light conditions and visual interference between the two layers and the reflected environment create a moiré effect in which individual identity and global market anonymity blend.

Jourdan & Müller + Benjamin Jourdan + ECE. City Point.

The facade causes a continually shifting, shimmering, alluring perception. Ben van Berkel (UN Studio), states this is a building for living design, not dead art.

The exterior renewal consists of the application of 4330 glass disks to the existing façade. These discs are treated with a special iridescent foil, which causes constant changes in the perception of the façade. At night, a special lighting scheme illuminates the discs by reflecting the dynamics of the weather conditions that happened during the day.

UN Studio / Van Berkel + Bos. Galleria Hall West.

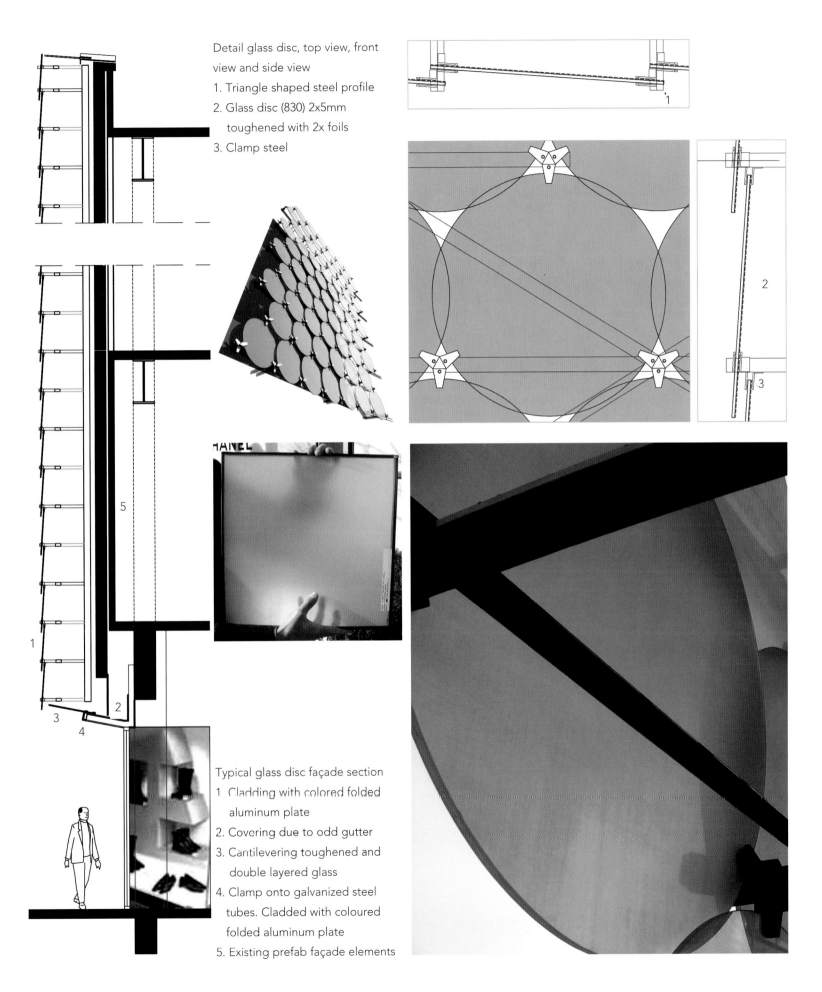

Detail glass disc, top view, front view and side view

1. Triangle shaped steel profile
2. Glass disc (830) 2x5mm toughened with 2x foils
3. Clamp steel

Typical glass disc façade section

1. Cladding with colored folded aluminum plate
2. Covering due to odd gutter
3. Cantilevering toughened and double layered glass
4. Clamp onto galvanized steel tubes. Cladded with coloured folded aluminum plate
5. Existing prefab façade elements

# GLASS BLOCK FACADES

This complex consists of two blocks located in an old industrial zone of the city centre. The street facade of both volumes is clad in stucco with balconies that overlook the road. The interior facade, offering greater privacy, looks over the garden and is built with glass blocks and large openings. Behind this facade, and between each apartment and the garden, there is a 3 m corridor that acts as a central space for the relaxation and encounters of the tenants. Daylight comes in through the glass facade, and at night the situation is reversed: the artificial light is projected to the exterior, converting the building into an enormous lighting element set in the garden.

Wiel Arets. Project for the Elderly.

The rectangular ground plan of the complex is divided into eight volumes that house the small residential units. These are set on a concrete plinth and offer a powerful silhouette against the disarticulated urban landscape of Hachioji, in Tokyo.

The functional programme was resolved with great simplicity: the apartments occupy the higher levels, within eight cubes measuring six metres, whose exterior walls combine glass blocks and aluminium sheeting.

Toshio Akimoto. Yakult Dormitory.

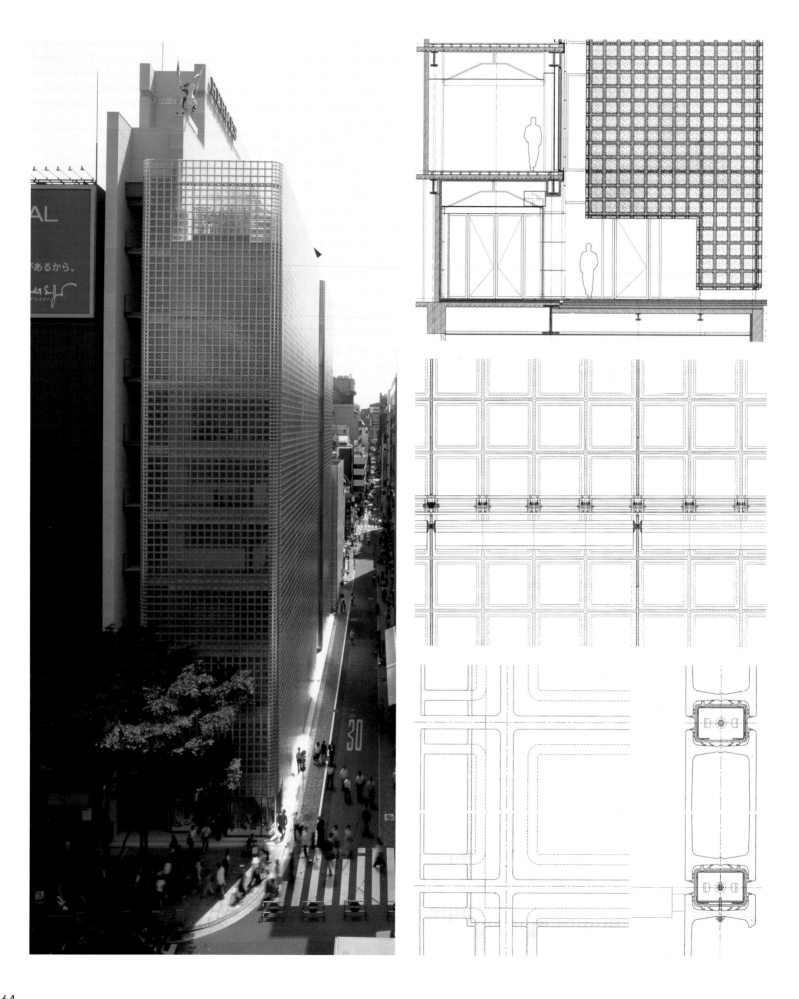

Renzo Piano Building Workshop. Maison Hermès.

Herzog & de Meuron. Prada Aoyama Epicenter. Tokyo.

# PLASTIC FACADES

The application of plastic as a constructive material is growing from two different points of view: one which values its expressive qualities and the other that exploits its low cost and industrial character.

Plastic as a material is understood to be formed primarily from synthetic polymer, to which all kinds of property modifiers can be added (stabilizers, foams, plastifiers...) as well as additives, which lower the cost of the product. The polymers are carbon-based, which effects the properties of the final product. The combustibility of polymers is a drawback that limits the use of plastics.

There are two large families of synthetic polymers: thermosets and thermoplastics.

Thermoset polymers are characterized by their hard surface and dimensional stability. The addition of reinforcing fibers to any plastic material increases its rigidity and resistance to impact and traction and reduces the transformation of the material when subjected to heat. Thermoset polymers include: phenoplasts, aminoplasts, synthetic resins and epoxies.

Thermoplastic polymers can be used to manufacture encasings with the required degree of opacity or transparency. Thermoplastic polymers include: cellulosic, vinyllic, ethylenic, styrenic, acetal, acryllic, carbonates and fluorates. Polyvinyl Chloride (PVC) is a vinyl belonging to the thermoplastics, which can be flexible or rigid.

When subjected to increases in temperature, the macromolecules of thermoplastics present states of deformation previous to carbonization, in contrast to thermosets.

The properties of polymers are highly varied due to the wide range of structural possibilities, both on a molecular and macromolecular level. They possess properties that are physical, mechanical, hygrothermal, optical-visual and are extremely durable.

The two faces of the building display totally opposite personalities: although balconies exist on both, the delicate aluminum balconies of the long façade gain a measure of privacy and are shielded from the direct sunlight by translucent polycarbonate screens, which visually unify the whole surface; in contraposition to this, the short façade is characterized by wide cantilevered balconies that project far into space, opening up or revealing the building's inner structural distribution.

TEN Arquitectos. Parque España Residential Euilcing.

This construction is built in situ with concrete so as to reach all interstices and clad in several layers which form a red plastic water-proof polyurethane membrane, turning the facade and the roof into a single element. The openings in the facade are emphasised by sections of extruded polystyrene.

Manuel Herz. "Legal / Illegal".

hobby a., Wolfgang Maul & Walter Schuster. Casa para Eva y Fritz.

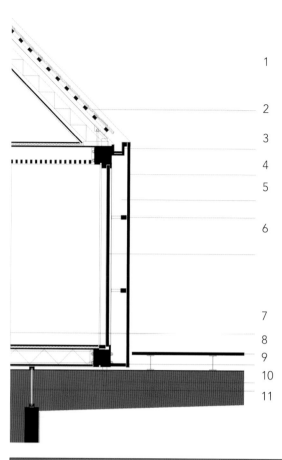

Section of double wall and roof

1. Clapboard roof
2. Internal gutter
3. Cladding (polycarbonate dual-wall) with breather hotels
4. Clearance
5. Substructure with spacers
6. Wall panels, Gluelam covered with OSB
7. Bracing wall
8. Terrace
9. Deal with ventilation holes
10. Steel anchoring
11. Fanlight

Florian Nagler Architekten. House and Studio Lang-Kröll.

The climbing grips spell "the Blind Facade" in Braille. A "door-scope" is placed the wrong way around in the main door. Normally used to see who is at the door, here it reveals the interior. This area receives an average of 134 rainy days a year, a fact which inspired the reinvention of spouts and cisterns, while the polyurethane skin lets the rain play sculptural tricks with the building.

Kalhöfer – Korschildgen. Fahrt ins Grüne.

177

# MIXED FACADES

After considering the different types of facades, we will conclude with mixed facades.

Mixed facades are those in which the skin is composed of several of the materials considered in the previous chapters. Of course, most buildings do not use a single material on the facade, but one tends to predominate and characterise the design.

A combination of materials, colours and textures offers greater possibilities for the composition of the building, differentiating planes and volumes, and even the different uses in the interior of the building.

# MIXED FACADES

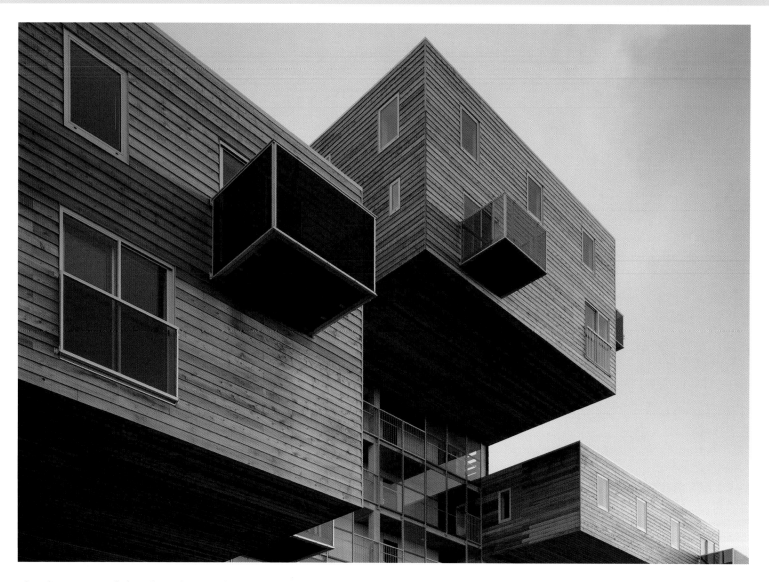

The dimensions of the plot - long and narrow - and the north-south orientation made it necessary to create a longitudinal volume and to adopt a module of 7.20 metres on the facade, since a deeper block with narrower dwellings did not seem feasible. To ensure sufficient exposure to the sun in the surroundings buildings, only 87 of the required hundred units could be housed in the block, so it was decided to add overhanging volumes on the north facade. These boxes -that stand out from the facade aligned to the street- are open at the sides in the east-west orientation (in Holland it is forbidden to orient dwellings only towards the north), offering views of the nearby polder. They are arranged without apparent order, creating different perspectives from the galleries of the different floors. These galleries are partially closed with glass, and some parts are left open to ventilate the rooms (kitchens and a small utility room) that give onto this facade. With the variations in the position of the windows and the different measures and materials of the balconies -in which different colours are used- each dwelling has its own character. Due to the regulations on fire and acoustic insulation, the overhanging structures had to be clad; they are finished in wood, like the south facade, contrasting with the glass and concrete surface of the galleries.

In the design of the openings, great richness and variety of forms and materials was necessary in order to provide the individuality required for each apartment. Thirteen of the hundred apartments are totally suspended from the north facade by means of a triangulated metal frame that absorbs the overhang. Each of these 13 apartments receives sunlight on the east and west facades.

The colour of the balcony was decided by the tenants, which explains the variety and the chromatic rhythm that governs the building.

MVRDV. 100 Wozoco's

181

The building is a long block parallel to the road that runs through the valley. The facade on the road side has views and sunlight, whereas the rear facade faces the north and the mountain. The end walls respond in their composition to similar principles: the west facade, the first that is seen when one approaches from the town, shows the thickness of the building, whereas the opposite wall, which gives straight onto the landscape, opens the building toward the exterior and transforms the end of the block into a sort of ship's bow.

The south facade expresses the differences in size between the rooms and combines the stone cladding of the larger surfaces with the zinc cladding of the overhanging elements. The north facade is clad in concrete blocks, a cheap material that creates a special tension with the sophisticated technology used in the lintels to allow the long horizontal openings.

A low wall of hollow bricks with thermal protection has simple guides attached halfway between the floor slabs. The veneer of San Vicente stone is 3 cm thick. The horizontal joint between the stones is 6 mm and the vertical one 4 mm. Water penetration is reduced by these narrow joints, the width of which is established by the type of fixing, the precision in the assembly and the calculated movement of the structure.

An interesting innovation in this work was the lattice of stone slats, consisting of folded panels of stainless steel to which the stone was attached.

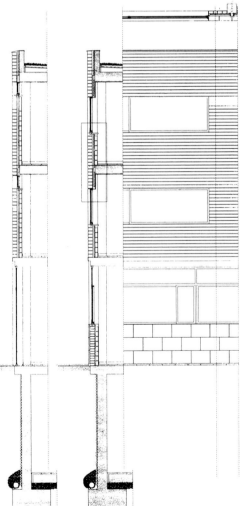

Josep. Lluis Mateo & Jaume Avellaneda. Residence for the elderly.

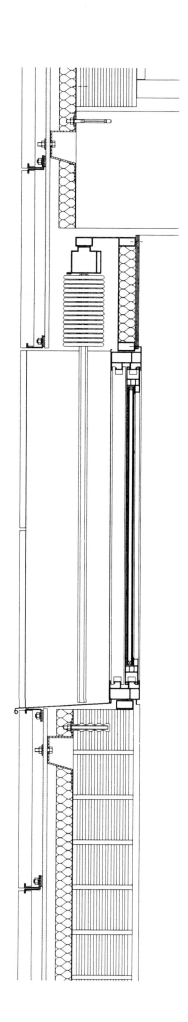
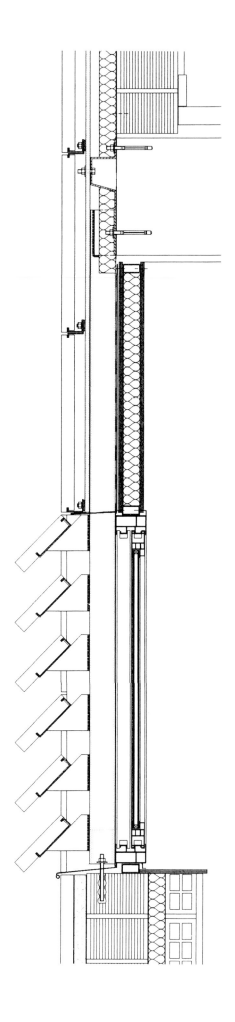

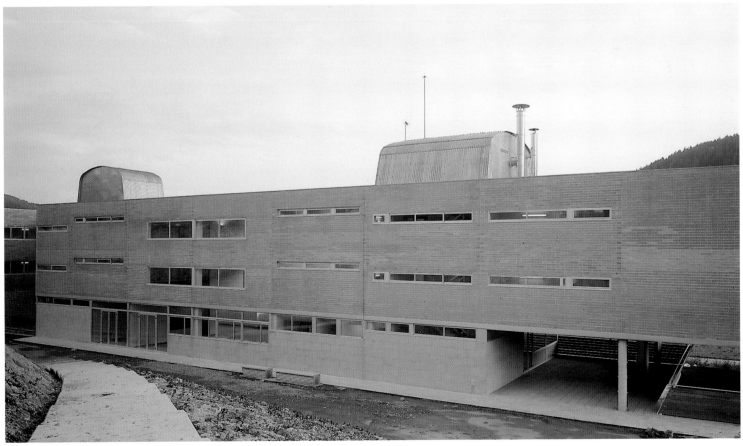

185

The apartment building consists of a linear block divided horizontally into three clearly differentiated parts: a plinth of offices and shops, a central volume with 26 apartments and a set of six large articulated villas that complete the volume. Though wrapped in a common volumetric shell, each of these parts expresses its relation to the exterior through the different openings and the different textures and materials.

The plinth has the function of direct connection with the immediate urban environment and with the remaining elements of the scheme. Finished in sturdy stone slates from the Ardennes region, it opens at the points corresponding to the shops and the four doorways, and is prolonged into the interior of the block to form the walls that delimit the gardens paces, the old villa and the car park.

The central volume is clad in panels of anthracite grey that create tight longitudinal strips of facade which are cut by the horizontal strips of the windows. The six villas that complete the building are presented as a sculptural combination of fragmentary and articulated volumes clad in red cedar. The three intermediate floors consist of a forceful rectangular volume with a rhythm of windows sunk and cut into the facade of concrete and anthracite grey.

The line of the roof is described through a sculptural combination of volumes clad in cedar, whose corners and recesses form luxurious terraces.

W. J. Neutelings. Apartment Complex "Prinsenhock".

This old two-storey stone farmhouse was a damp place without running water that urgently needed restoration. The work had to be carried out without spoiling the transparent typology of the existing structure. The building is accessed through a surprisingly large entrance located in the centre of a stone wall. An annex in larch wood on the west side is now the sunniest part of this solid stone house.

Architekturbüro Gasparin & Meier. Badehaus Ebenberger.

The ground plan of the lower level is square, whereas that of the higher levels is semicircular. This difference is also reflected in the materials used for the exterior cladding of each level: white painted brick at street level and grooved metal plate on the first and second floors.

The facade giving onto the street seems to be a continuation of the ground floor, but the rear part of the dwelling is resolved in a different way, in a semi-circle.

Linda Searl & Joseph Valerio. Ohio House.

189

The light-weight cedar wood guesthouse hovers over the ground and cantilevers off of the garage, which is constructed using rough stone collected from the site. A glass façade and terrace take advantage of the spectacular surroundings.

Archi-Tectonics. Gypsy Trail Guesthouse.

The main structural component is structural insulated panels (SIPS), which provide the envelope and roof. The wedge shape that encloses the ramp is clad in red anodized aluminum panels, and the rest of the exterior is finished in Aquatec, a plywood with a natural preservative that protects the wood while allowing it to change over time.

M. J. Neal. Ramp House.

The principal facade is defined by a distinctive combination of patterned glass and metal, which defines the exterior of the building and filters the natural light reaching the interior. The identical overhangs along both sides of the building emphasize the strong horizontal linearity of the construction.

Andrej Kalamar. Shopping Center in Lendava.

Emmanuel Combarel Dominique Marrec Architectes. Social Housing for Students in Argenteuil.

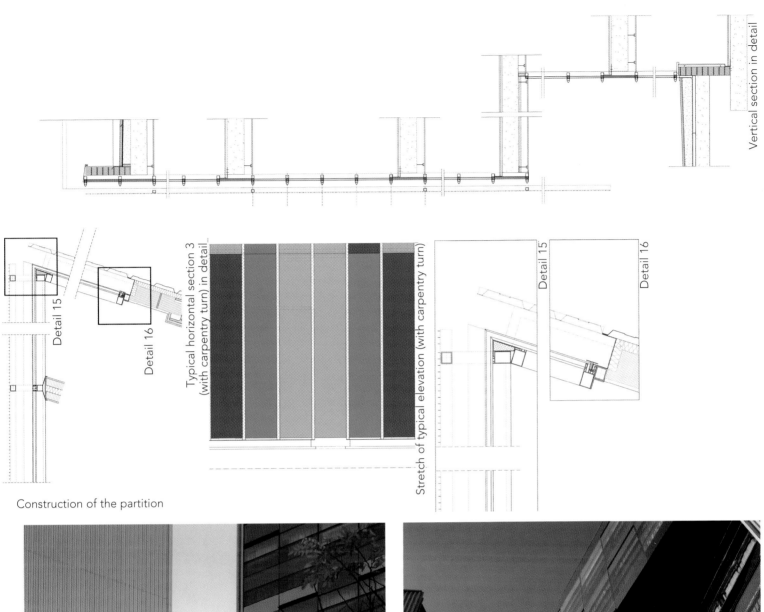

Vertical section in detail

Detail 15

Detail 16

Detail 15

Detail 16

Typical horizontal section 3
(with carpentry turn) in detail

Stretch of typical elevation (with carpentry turn)

Construction of the partition

ADD + Arquitectura, Manuel Bailo & Rosa Rull. Hotel ciutat d'Igualada.

# FACADE ENCLOSURES, OPENINGS

Windows are a particularly important feature of the outer walls of a building because their thermal and acoustic insulation is often lower than that of the walls in which they are set, and they may cause leaking of water through their joints and damp due to condensation.

A further aspect of windows is the insulation that they provide against external noise.

One of the fundamental characteristics of openings that we will deal with in this chapter is their arrangement on the facade to create different compositions, which together with the elements that protect them, such as blinds and shutters, give each building its personality.

A general classification of windows would include fixed lights, folding casements, sliding windows and pivoted sashes. There are also windows with louvred shutters and folding windows.

The joinery of the windows may be of wood, steel, aluminium or PVC, though the new materials that are coming onto the market offer better protection against moisture and wind.

Additional elements on the facade include systems of shade and protection that control the degree of lighting, sunlight and ventilation, partial reduction of views, and protection from forced entry.

These elements include blinds, slats, awnings, lattices and protective elements such as grilles and railings.

# OPENINGS (WINDOWS)

The main facades of this residential complex are of rubble with exterior insulation and a fine stucco finish with a uniform colour that forms a smooth skin wrapping the geometric volume of the building. The dark chestnut colour of the outer walls is set against the bright orange of the walls of the court, generating a rich chromatic effect of contrasts in a space that varies with the changes of light during the day.

The large windows run from floor to ceiling on the facades and are like enormous eyes looking over the lake and the park. They have a wide aluminium frame that houses the blinds, runners and wooden joinery. Seen from the exterior, these windows have no external protection or railings.

The free arrangement of the openings corresponds to the different types of apartments.

Annette Gigon & Mike Guyer. Residential Complex in Kilchberg.

As the architects wished to design a facade that was as transparent as possible with windows of great height, they had to devise some construction tricks to give the building sufficient solidity. The complete transparency of the facades is achieved through openings that run from floor to ceiling, and the metal joinery of the doors and windows acts as a loadbearing element. The only details of finishes on the facade are the sturdy wooden shutters that cover the concrete sections.

Bjarne Mastenbroek & MVRDV. Double House Utrecht.

A double height window with a southern aspect offers impressive views of the valley. The balcony, which is the only element that stands out from the facade, was deliberately covered with zinc oxide to make it more striking. The remaining materials are the habitual ones of this area of the Alps: exposed concrete, American pine, glass and metal plate for the exterior, white render for the interior walls and solid wood for the roof and flooring. The large window is hermetically insulated to minimise heating costs.

Margarethe Heubacher-Sentobe. House for a Musician.

Hans Peter Wörndl. Gucklhupf.

207

208

Cino Zucchi. House "D" / Ex-Junghans factory urban renewal.

# SLIDING WALLS

The material expression of the facades of this programme partly blurs the built mass. The three buildings of which the scheme is composed were approached in a similar way, by closing the north facade with a stone veneer with sharp horizontal incisions. The rest of the facades have a double skin consisting of red stucco divided by vertical openings from floor to ceiling in the interior, and an outer skin separated by 60 cm from the inner one, consisting of panels of wooden slats that can be moved freely according to the needs of the occupants.

These mobile panels provide an exterior space around all the dwellings that extends the interior space visually. The terrace of the living room can be understood as an interior or an exterior according to the position of the panels.

Constructive details of the sliding window

1. Drip edge of folded aluminium plate
2. Sliding aluminum runners
3. Aluminum frame of blind
4. 50x30 mm Iroko wood slats
5. Stainless steel handrail
6. 6+6 Stadip glass panels, as railing
7. 90x30 mm floorboards of Iroko wood with open joints
8. Frame of blinds and panes formed by L-100/8 with 60x8 welded plate
9. 240x12x8 welded connection plate to two 160x60x8 plates screwed with perforated supports
10. Bracket formed by 1/2 IPE-200 welded to continuous L-100/8 anchored to the slab

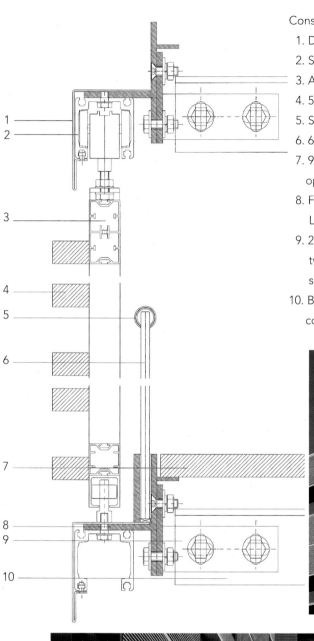

Jaume Bach & Gabriel Mora. Illa Fleming.

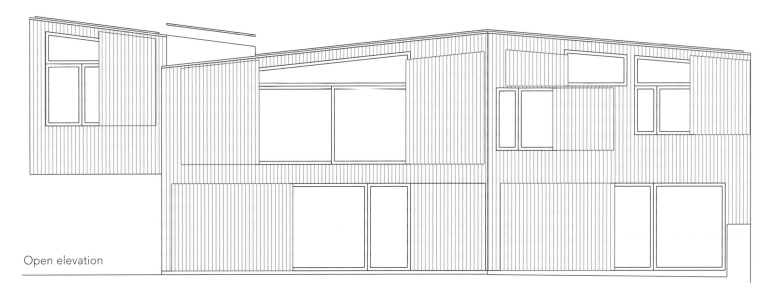

Open elevation

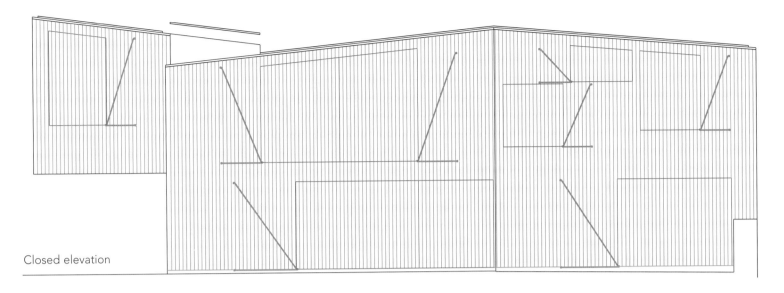

Closed elevation

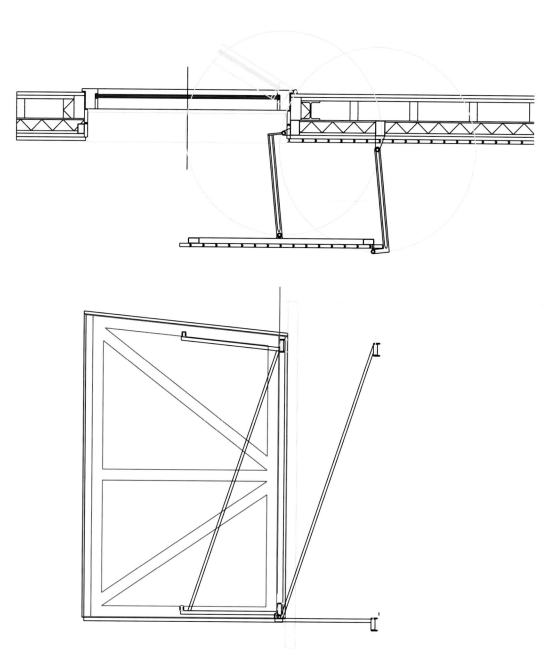

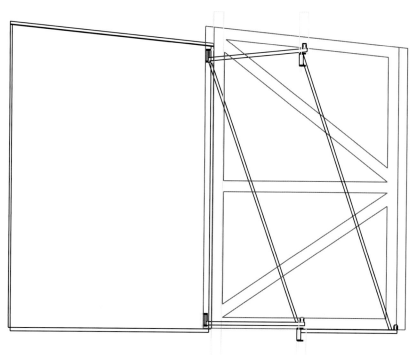

The shutters are thus supported at two points and balanced by a third. A prototype measuring 14 square inches (35 sq cm) in surface area with 16-inch-long (40 cm) arms was perfected in the workshop. Having achieved satisfactory results, a life-sized model that multiplied the size by 20 and the arm by 4 was put to the test.

Placed in an austere row, these four volumes have a rectangular floor plan and look over the river on one of their side elevations. Completely covered with laminated marine wood, the buildings develop a simple and functional language that refers to the local tradition. The enormous sliding shutters give the image, in the distance, of the doors of a large barn. As one approaches, one sees that in fact they contain apartments, and a further examination shows that they are rooms for the elderly.

The transparent outer skin also reveals the geometry of the wooden structure. The openings are protected from the excessive solar radiation by large sliding shutters. The buildings, whose structure is of reinforced concrete, are covered by a skin of untreated pine wood, which will go grey in the course of time.

Mahler, Günster & Fuchs. Residence in the Black Forest.

218

The dwellings receive a great deal of natural light through generous openings in the facade. A system of sliding wooden blinds of red cedar filters the incoming light. The wooden blinds and the horizontal strips of prefabricated concrete help to compose the façade formally.

Philippe Madec. Dwellings in Paris 20.

# THE FOLDING FACADE

In terms of volume, this scheme consists of a plinth that supports two buildings (the hotel and the apartment block), which is clad in dark grey enamelled glass in the opaque areas, creating a similar effect to that of a normal glass window.

In contrast to this "transparent" base, the upper part is clad in matt glass on the exterior. Both the open spaces and the closed volumes shine through a matt external envelope.

Due to the modular use, to the layout of the windows, to the matt glass and to the folding shutters, the facades look more like a code than a composition.

Depending on the use of the adjacent spaces, the facade consists of a series of layers of matt glass, transparent glass, and screens of thermal or solar insulation in several combinations.

To protect the interior from excessive sunlight, sliding aluminium shutters were incorporated in the facade. It is as if the envelope of the building opened in an ever-changing motif.

The two white housing volumes show the composition based on floor-to-ceiling panels. The use of shutters over the glass panes produces a facade whose appearance changes continually according to the use of the housing and the climate, forming musical variations on the same lattice subject. The scheme has thus been designed with attention to the environment, in which it stands self-assured.

Bürg n Nissen Wentzlaff. Housing in M..tt nz.

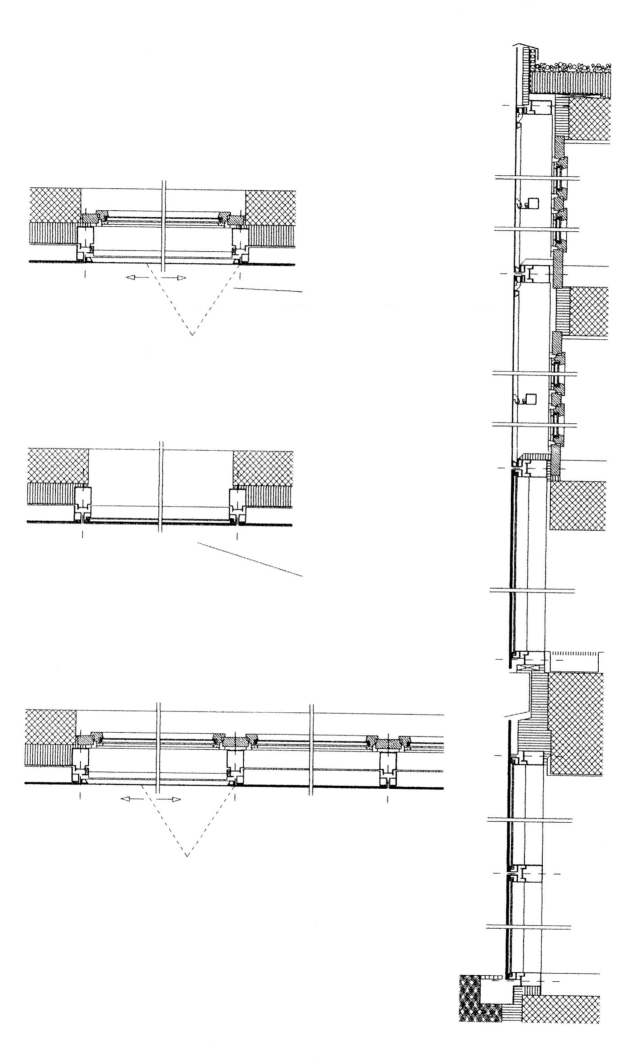

The street facade is totally glazed and is protected by a cast iron curtain that can be folded element by element. The undulating openings give the curtain a fluid and textile feeling. Whereas the construction of the facade leaves the central space of the dwelling behind, its heavy material provides protection against the unpleasant noise on this side of the street.

The photograph shows the absolute independence of the structure, which only adapts to the needs of the residents.

Sánchez Higuera, S.C. Hotel Condesa.

Herzog & de Meuron. Fünf Höfe.

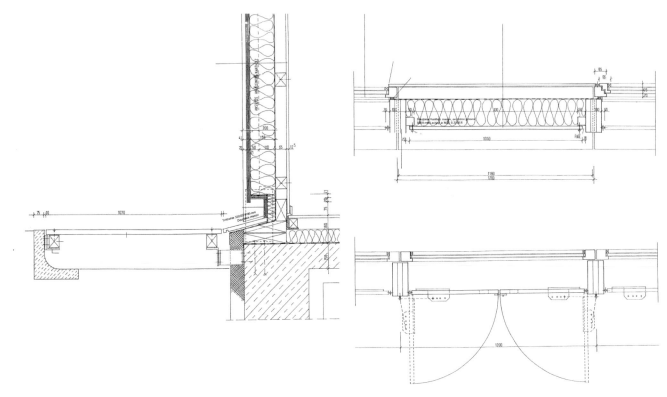

A rural approach was used for this dwelling, which is interpreted as a technically innovative residential building that has an experimental function in its current situation. The facade is a decorative concrete wall with a great wooden door at the rear. The front of the building consists of a structure of laminated wood posts with a panel of Betoplan (epoxy-coated plywood). The panels are both fixed, with red fixings to provide contrast, or moveable with wooden shutters over the windows.

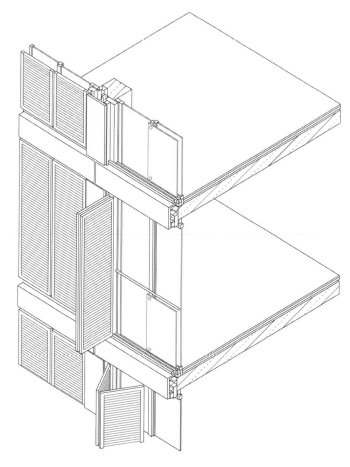

Alexander Reichel. Urban Villa in Kassel.

231

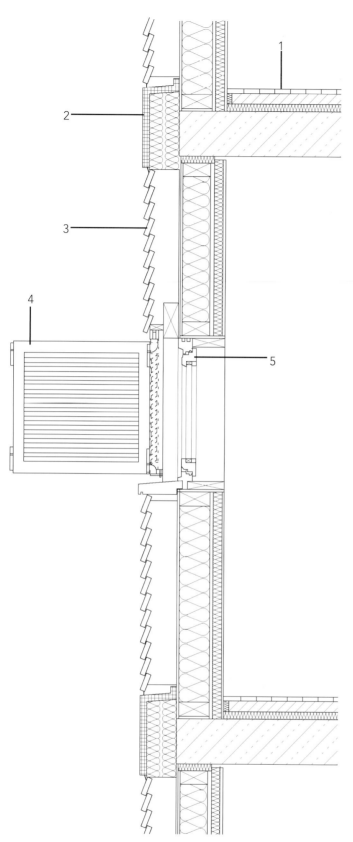

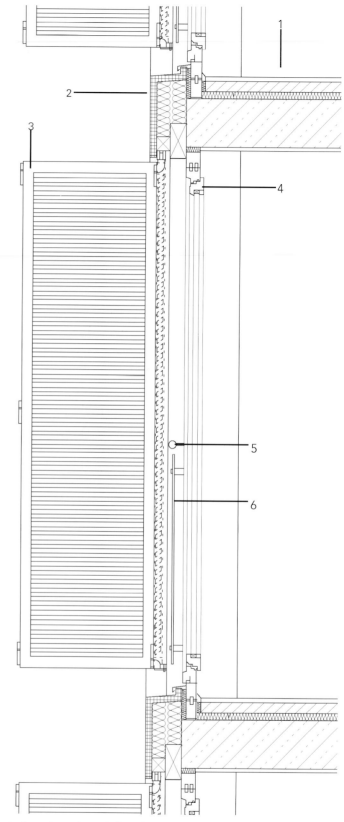

Vertical section of east-west timber wall

1. 22 mm industrial-quality parquet
2. 30 mm glass-fibre-reinforced concrete
3. 22/80 mm larch shiplap boarding
4. 50 mm untreated larch sliding-folding shutters
5. Larch window, clear varnished

Vertical section of south facade

1. 22 mm industrial-quality parquet
2. 30 mm glass-fibre-reinforced concrete
3. 50 mm untreated larch sliding-folding shutters
4. Larch window, clear varnished
5. 30 mm diam. polished stainless-steel safety rail
6. 12 mm safety glass balustrade

Detail horizontal section

1. Larch casement, clear varnished
2. Untreated larch sliding-folding shutter
3. 30 mm glass-fibre-reinforced concrete adhesive-fixed
4. Cranking handle for sliding-folding shutter
5. 240/240 mm in-situ concrete column

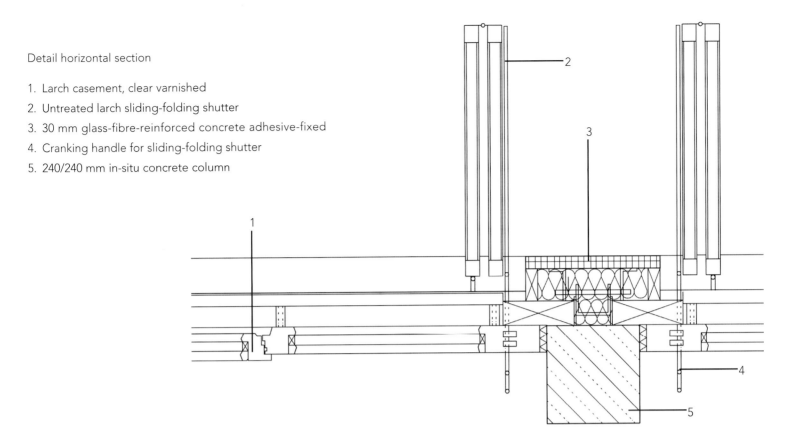

# BLINDS AND CURTAINS

The apartments are grouped around a court that opens on the south side to the adjoining plot. This side opening is not only intended to let the light and sunshine into the apartments, but also to take advantage of the greenery of a large tree situated on the adjoining plot.

The apartments all look towards the central court. The outer walls are totally glazed and protected with wooden roller blinds.

Herzog & De Meuron. Apartamentos en una parcela larga y estrecha.

234

Several treatments of the glass and the careful study of the shade and the incoming light manipulate this relationship according to the brief and its orientation.

The volumetrics and the different types of glazing and other solar protections dominate the exterior appearance of the dwelling.

A surface floating over the ground serves as a base for the glazed volume that is protected with interior cloth curtains and exterior metal curtains.

Rem Koolhas. Dutch House.

235

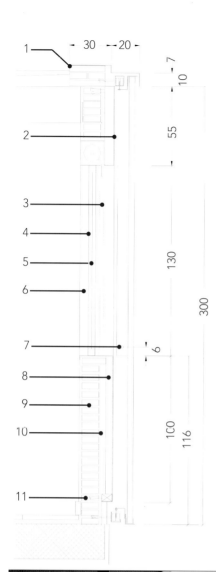

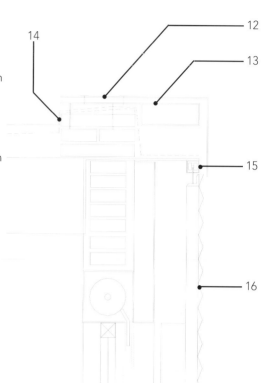

Detail 1:

1. Folded galvanized steel sheet, e=4 mm
2. Aluminum sheet polished in its original color, e=1 mm
3. Aluminum blind polished in its original color
4. Aluminum joinery Mm9/Vm10
5. Glass, e=4 mm
6. Aluminum sheet polished in its original color, e=1 mm
7. Aluminum bar, d=20 mm
8. Polystyrene thermal insulation, e= 4 cm
9. Brick wall
10. Air cavity
11. Steel hook

Detail 2:

12. Galvanised steel corner sheet.
13. Sheet supporting profile.
14. Waterproof felt underhand.
15. Sliding door horizontal, 40 x 40 mm.
16. Deployee galvanised steel mesh.

José Morales Sánchez & Juan González Mariscal. Housing in San Jerónimo.

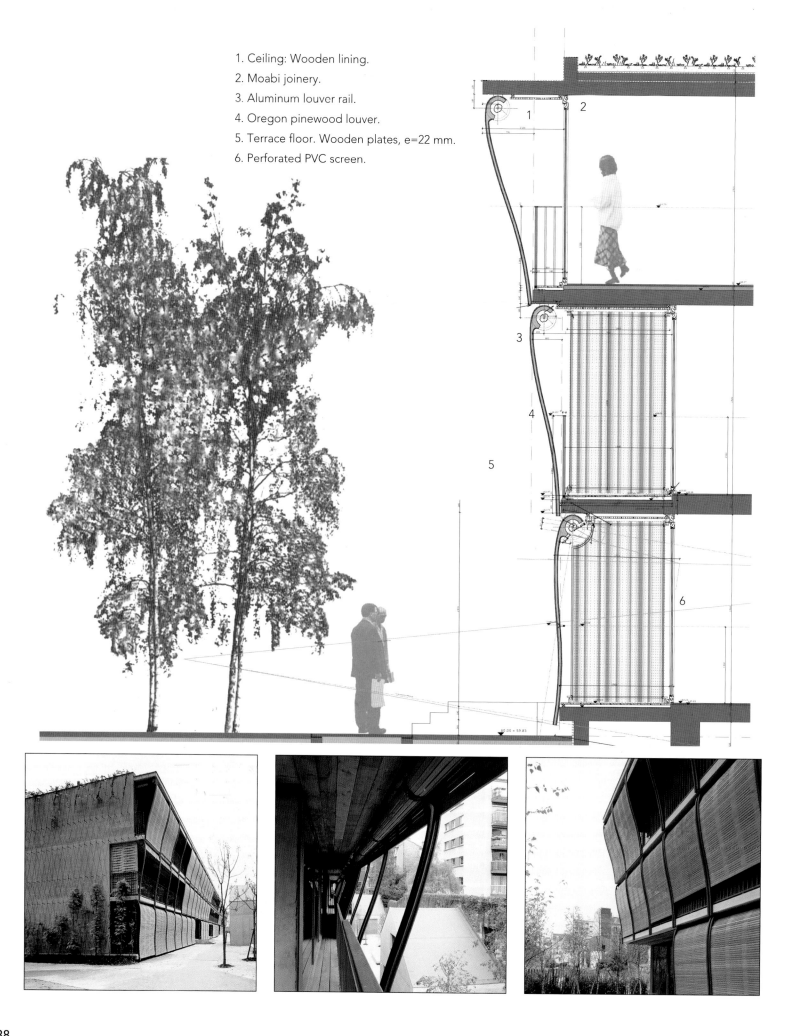

1. Ceiling: Wooden lining.
2. Moabi joinery.
3. Aluminum louver rail.
4. Oregon pinewood louver.
5. Terrace floor. Wooden plates, e=22 mm.
6. Perforated PVC screen.

J. Herzog & P. de Meuron. Housing in Rue des Suisses.

239